Praise for Mission Possible

D0642363

"The authors describe their schools as places defined by [...]
Success Academy, I can attest to that. If we are going t[...]
living in poverty, we need to create more opportunities t[...]
places like Success Academies. This book does just that, taking the best practices from
the Success Academies and creating a framework for educators, parents, and
policy-makers to learn from their successes."
—**Sen. Michael F. Bennet**, Colorado

"*Mission Possible* is a testament to what can be achieved in public education when the
focus shifts to improving rigor in instruction and continuing education for teachers and
principals."
—**Doug Lemov**, managing director, Uncommon Schools; author, *Teach Like a
Champion*

"It is long past time to end the needless conflict between district-run and charter
schools, and instead spend our time working together and learning from each other.
That is why this book is so important and so timely. We need to learn from the best
practices of our successful public schools, whether district-run or charter, and reflect on
ways to improve public education for the benefit of all our kids."
—**Tom Boasberg**, superintendent, Denver Public Schools

"Among the most promising urban charter schools, like the Success Academies, we see
sustaining cultures where adults focus on student learning and performance and on
supporting each other. As always, we need an intimate glimpse into how those cultures
build and grow stronger, and what is the 'stuff' that goes on within classrooms. This
book gives us that glimpse, in ways that can benefit all schools."
—**Andres Alonso**, CEO, Baltimore City Public School System

"Success Academy schools are not just great public schools, they are the wave of the
future. But great schools can't be left to chance. The stakes are too high. Just as we
expect children of all backgrounds to learn more every day in school, *Mission Possible*
shows us how a culture of continuous improvement also allows teachers themselves the
gratification of continuing to learn and grow professionally each and every day to better
meet student needs."
—**Eli Broad**, founder, The Broad Foundations

MISSION POSSIBLE

How the Secrets of Success Academies Can Work in Any School

Eva Moskowitz
Arin Lavinia

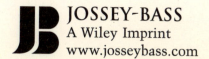

JOSSEY-BASS
A Wiley Imprint
www.josseybass.com

Copyright © 2012 by John Wiley & Sons, Inc. All rights reserved.

Published by Jossey-Bass
A Wiley Imprint
One Montgomery Street, Suite 1200, San Francisco, CA 94104-4594—www.josseybass.com

No part of this publication may be reproduced, stored in a retrieval system, or transmitted in any form or by any means, electronic, mechanical, photocopying, recording, scanning, or otherwise, except as permitted under Section 107 or 108 of the 1976 United States Copyright Act, without either the prior written permission of the publisher, or authorization through payment of the appropriate per-copy fee to the Copyright Clearance Center, Inc., 222 Rosewood Drive, Danvers, MA 01923, 978-750-8400, fax 978-646-8600, or on the Web at www.copyright.com. Requests to the publisher for permission should be addressed to the Permissions Department, John Wiley & Sons, Inc., 111 River Street, Hoboken, NJ 07030, 201-748-6011, fax 201-748-6008, or online at www.wiley.com/go/permissions.

Limit of Liability/Disclaimer of Warranty: While the publisher and author have used their best efforts in preparing this book, they make no representations or warranties with respect to the accuracy or completeness of the contents of this book and specifically disclaim any implied warranties of merchantability or fitness for a particular purpose. No warranty may be created or extended by sales representatives or written sales materials. The advice and strategies contained herein may not be suitable for your situation. You should consult with a professional where appropriate. Neither the publisher nor author shall be liable for any loss of profit or any other commercial damages, including but not limited to special, incidental, consequential, or other damages. Readers should be aware that Internet Web sites offered as citations and/or sources for further information may have changed or disappeared between the time this was written and when it is read.

Jossey-Bass books and products are available through most bookstores. To contact Jossey-Bass directly call our Customer Care Department within the U.S. at 800-956-7739, outside the U.S. at 317-572-3986, or fax 317-572-4002.

Wiley publishes in a variety of print and electronic formats and by print-on-demand. Some material included with standard print versions of this book may not be included in e-books or in print-on-demand. If this book refers to media such as a CD or DVD that is not included in the version you purchased, you may download this material at **http://booksupport.wiley.com**. For more information about Wiley products, visit **www.wiley.com**.

Library of Congress Cataloging-in-Publication Data
Moskowitz, Eva S.
  Mission possible : how the secrets of the success academies can work in any school / Eva Moskowitz, Arin Lavinia.
       p. cm.
  Includes bibliographical references and index.
  ISBN 978-1-118-16728-1 (pbk.), 978-1-118-16728-1 (ebk.), 978-1-118-23962-9 (ebk.), 978-1-118-26422-5 (ebk.)
  1. School improvement programs—New York (State)—New York—Case studies. 2. Academic achievement—New York (State)—New York—Case studies. 3. Charter schools—New York (State)—New York—Case studies. 4. Harlem Success Academy (New York, N.Y.) I. Lavinia, Arin, 1977- II. Title.
  LB2822.83.N7M67 2012
  371.2'07097471—dc23
                                                                          2012010374

Printed in the United States of America
FIRST EDITION
PB Printing   10 9 8 7 6 5 4 3 2 1

CONTENTS

To our indefatigable director of instruction, Paul Fucaloro; our hardworking and talented faculty; and our nine extraordinary principals, Jackie Albers, Jim Manly, Richard Seigler, Danique Loving, Stacey Apatov, Michele Caracappa, Vanessa Bangser, Monica Burress, and Carrie Roby

This book would not have been possible without the generous support of the Ford Foundation and its president, Luis Ubiñas.

LIST OF VIDEO CLIPS

Please note: For the e-book version, the video content can be accessed online at www.wiley.com/go/missionpossiblevideos. When prompted, use access code 67281.

MISSION POSSIBLE

INTRODUCTION

It sounds like a pipe dream: open a public elementary school in the middle of Harlem, take all comers through a random lottery, and within three years win recognition as the top charter in New York City and one of the very best public schools in all of New York State.

It's fact, not fiction. It's what we did with the first Success Academy Harlem and now are doing with eight more Success Academies in Harlem, the Bronx, Brooklyn, and the Upper West Side of Manhattan.

The students in Harlem, the Bronx, and Brooklyn are almost all minorities, the majority of whom live below the poverty line. Their parents seek to escape from failing district schools and to send their kids to college. You might have seen some of their stories in the documentaries *The Lottery* and *Waiting for Superman*.

We're making that hope a reality against long odds. We think we're on to something, and we want to share our story and describe how we created such successful schools where the common wisdom said they couldn't exist.

It may sound odd to hear educators talking so much about "beating the odds." But that's what we do. Great teachers are in the odds-beating business. When we do our jobs well, we alter the lives of the children and families we serve. We give children an opportunity to live the American dream that the odds-makers suggested they couldn't possibly have.

Walk into any one of the Success Academies in New York City and enter a new kind of school, a colorful, enchanting place where the kids we call "scholars" are doing phenomenal things thanks to their hard work, great teaching by exceptionally well-trained teachers, and the support of parents willing to do whatever it takes to get their children a world-class education.

Our talented educators and committed staff fully understand the reality of what we're dealing with: were it not for these dynamic schools, and the ability of our families to exercise choice over what school their child attends, most of our young scholars would have been consigned to zoned district schools that offer little hope for a bright future.

We're talking about schools in which most students are not on track to graduate, in which success itself is an anomaly, whether it is on the third-grade reading test or in mastering the skills required to attend a college or university. Beating the odds means shattering that trajectory and starting all over with much higher expectations about what is possible for students. It means offering hope for a better life to students who otherwise would be forced to attend the kinds of failing public schools where dreams usually go to die. It means not giving up on the romantic notion that public education can do better for these students— much better.

This is the world that Eva Moskowitz envisioned in 2005 when she took off her hat as elected city official and became a charter school founder and not-for-profit entrepreneur.

She was motivated by a deep commitment to educational justice and educational excellence. As a former college history professor and city councilwoman, Eva believed passionately that children deserved and needed a much better education than most were getting in the public schools of New York City and indeed in cities, suburbs, and towns across the country. And she knew better than most people how destructive the schools in neighborhoods like Harlem could be, because she attended them herself as a child growing up in New York City in the 1970s. Her parents, both college professors, taught their daughter after school what she should have learned in the classroom. Later she attended the elite Stuyvesant High School, regarded and respected as one of the best public schools in America. But even Stuyvesant, Eva knew, wasn't anywhere near as academically rigorous as it needed to be. It was packed with students whose parents, like her own, were able to academically compensate for the weak education they were getting from the city's public schools.

When Eva had children of her own, she wanted them to have the kind of high-caliber public education that all parents want for their kids. As a public school parent, she was frustrated with what she saw in the schools. Even at well-regarded public schools she saw a lack of rigor and a "pretty good is good enough" attitude. And then there were the absurdities. Despite the $24 billion city education budget, parents were required by schools to bring in toilet paper, paper towels, and Windex. In less affluent neighborhoods, kids simply went without. Whether looking at high school graduation rates, test scores, or student writing, Eva saw firsthand that we were miseducating and grossly undereducating children.

Eva successfully ran for the New York City Council in 1999 because she wanted to change the broken education system that served 1.1 million schoolchildren. Once in office, she jousted with the city bureaucracy and unions over mismanagement; misplaced priorities; lax standards; and crazy work rules that left science labs without equipment, art classes without art supplies, buildings without lights working, and restrooms without toilet paper in a system that spends a whopping $19,000-plus a year per student.

Week after week, Eva held public hearings that probed into every corner of school operations. She demanded answers and often ran into brick walls and powerful forces, like Mayor Michael Bloomberg and teachers union leaders, who continually urged her to lower her expectations for public education. But after six years in office, and a bruising defeat for the position of Manhattan borough president, she left the city council frustrated that the schools were nowhere near where they needed to be.

Eva possessed the confidence to think she could create from scratch elementary schools that were much better than the dysfunctional ones she had visited as chair of the council's Education Committee. She jumped into the public charter school arena at a time when education visionaries and pioneers, such as Dave Levin and Mike Feinberg at KIPP, were showing the world that bigger and better things were possible for students whom many had long ago written off. Eva borrowed what she saw as the best approaches from successful schools of all types—public, charter, parochial, and private—and in August 2006 Success Academy opened the first Success Academy Harlem on 118th Street and Lenox Avenue, located on one floor of a building shared with P.S. 149, the Sojourner Truth School. Eva herself worked as both the founder of the network and the principal for the first two years. She consulted with every successful education expert she could find, and studied every style of instruction under the sun.

Eva searched high and low to find someone who shared her desire to significantly raise the bar by designing a world-class reading and writing curriculum. She stumbled across Arin Lavinia, who was the first educator Eva had ever met who shared her incredibly high standards for reading and writing. When Eva asked Arin how many of the children in her schools could be expected to achieve mastery, Arin replied, "All of them." Arin, who had been a classroom teacher in New York City's District 2, and who had become a staff developer for the Teachers College Reading and Writing Project, was working nationally as a literacy consultant when her path crossed with Eva's. In 2009 she came on board as Success Academy's director of literacy. We quickly began the task of customizing our own reading and writing curriculum, which we often jokingly describe as "balanced literacy on steroids." Our approach is built around great books and the power of ideas, with scholars learning from the get-go how to think critically and express ideas elegantly, not just parrot back abstruse skills and strategies.

We plan eventually to run forty K–8 schools with 25,000 students. Currently 3,500 students attend our nine schools, with five more schools slated to open in summer 2012.

We don't cherry-pick our young scholars. Most are eligible for free- and reduced-price lunches. Fifteen percent are in special education. One in ten is still learning English. And, like other charters, we teach them with about 15 to 20 percent fewer dollars from the city and state than traditional or district public schools receive.

In spring 2009 our first scholars were completing third grade, and they took New York State's standardized tests in math and English language arts for the first time. The scores they posted were astonishing. Every child—100 percent—was proficient or better in math, and most scored at the advanced level. Ninety-five percent passed the English exam. We were the top-scoring charter in New York City. Only 31 of the 3,500 schools in the entire state scored higher.

So what's our secret? How do we do it?

First and foremost we focus on the grown-ups, not the children. We believe the adults in the school—principals and teachers—hold the keys to educational excellence. If they step up their performance, and if they set the bar high enough and truly believe that the children can rise to their expectations, then they can propel these students forward with lightning speed.

This is a radical, startling idea in the slow-to-change world of public education. But it is the touchstone of our beliefs, and we see it affirmed every day by the results in our joyful, rigorous classrooms.

Our scholars and their parents have been ready for everything we threw at them and more. Students attend class almost nine hours a day (7:45 a.m. to 4:30 p.m) and stay for an hour of after-school tutoring if needed; and some are back again on Saturday mornings. They bring homework assignments home each night and clamor for more.

We give our teachers extraordinary amounts of training, time, and resources to develop their professional skills. We provide coaching and mentoring to a degree unheard of in regular public schools. Teachers get about three preparation periods a day. The children spend three hours daily learning to become voracious readers and great writers because we believe that literacy is the key to learning. We couldn't find a literacy curriculum that fit our vision, so we've fine-tuned a reading curriculum of our own, which we call THINK Literacy.

Introduction to THINK Literacy and Success Academy Clip 1

This video shows THINK Literacy and our incredible teachers and scholars in action across grades at Success Academies. It offers a window into what's possible when schools put **critical thinking,** rigor, and grown-ups front and center.

In the chapters that follow we're going to take you on an extended trip inside the Success Academies. We'll show you THINK Literacy in action, and take you through some of the coaching and study sessions that our principals and teachers do together. We'll show you what we mean by doing things *fast,* a core value at Success Academies. You'll see how we help adults change and improve their practice fast, as well as the incredible scholar learning that occurs when teachers get better every day. We will visit schools, with a focus on the adults, and expose you to new areas of leverage for increasing the quality of student learning. We'll show you that this work is hard and, no less important, fun.

Pardon us if we shoot from the hip a little bit, but that's our style. We do everything with a sense of urgency. There is no time to waste if our scholars are to get where they need to go.

So take a close look at what we're doing at Success Academies. We encourage you to try it yourself. If you're a teacher or principal, we'll show you how we study and prepare lessons together, and the results we get from lots of coaching and feedback in real time. If you're a parent, we'll show you what to look for in your child's school and classroom. If you're an education reformer, we'll show you what policies need to change to support world-class schooling.

Most of all, we want you to believe as we do that the answer to America's school problems is not smaller class sizes or pay-for-performance or any of the other carrots and sticks that have been tried over the past quarter century with little to show. The answer is getting the adults to step up their game, giving them the training and help they need, and setting the bar far higher for everyone than anyone dreamed possible in public schools.

Welcome inside the Success Academies.

CHAPTER ONE

WHY?

What's Wrong with American Schools?

How can it be that in the United States more than a million teenagers—one in four—leave high school for the streets each year?[1]

How can it be that more than 60 percent of all students and nearly 80 percent of black and Hispanic students in fourth, eighth, and twelfth grade are reading and doing math below grade level?[2]

How can it be that a third of all fourth graders can't read at even a basic level?[3]

And why is it that things get worse the longer our students stay in school? Our nine-year-olds score in the top quarter on international tests in math, reading, and science. By age fifteen they've fallen to the bottom half.[4]

We used to be the world leader in graduating kids from high school. Now twenty-five of the world's thirty-four large industrialized nations have higher high school graduation rates than the United States.[5]

Not long ago we set the pace in sending students to college. Now we're thirteenth in the world—not because our college attendance rates have dropped, but because other countries have expanded opportunity and postsecondary capacity faster than we have.[6]

And it isn't just that we have more poor kids (one in five American kids grows up in poverty) and more minorities.[7] The gaps in learning between rich and poor are lower in numerous other countries, many of which also have large numbers of minority and immigrant students.

Sadly, we kid ourselves into thinking that this is an inner-city problem or a poverty problem or a black problem. The reality is that mediocrity is a pandemic in American education. Our schools, as philanthropist Bill Gates put it in a recent speech to the National Urban League, "range from outstanding to outrageous."[8]

The management consulting firm McKinsey & Company, in an analysis of the 2006 results for the Program for International Student Assessment (PISA) administered by the Organisation for Economic Co-operation and Development (OECD) to fifteen-year-olds in dozens of countries, concluded, "The facts here demonstrate that lagging achievement in the United States is not merely an issue for poor children attending schools in poor neighborhoods; instead, it affects most children in most schools."[9]

McKinsey also calculated that GDP would have been between $1 trillion and $2 trillion higher *each year* if the United States had closed the gap between its educational achievement levels and those of such top-performing nations as Finland and Korea.

Scholars from Stanford University, Harvard University, and the University of Munich recently compared the math scores of American eighth and ninth graders with the scores of kids around the world. Their conclusion: "The percentages of high-achieving math students in the U.S.—and most of its individual states—are shockingly below those of many of the world's leading industrialized nations. Results for many states are at the level of developing countries."[10]

According to the same study, only 6 percent of all U.S. students (and only 8 percent of white students) reached the advanced level. Sixteen countries, from Canada to Switzerland to Finland to Hong Kong to Taiwan, had two to four times that percentage of advanced students. "The only members of the Organisation for Economic Co-operation and Development . . . that produced a smaller percentage of advanced math students than the U.S. were Spain, Italy, Israel, Portugal, Greece, Turkey, Chile and Mexico."[11]

In Massachusetts, our top state, 11 percent of students were advanced, but even if every American student knew that much math we'd still trail four-teen countries. "The lowest ranking states—West Virginia, New Mexico, and Mississippi—have a smaller percentage of high-performing students than do Ser-bia and Uruguay (although they do edge out Romania, Brazil, and Kyrgyzstan)," the study said. In Mississippi, only 2 percent of students with a college-educated parent scored at the advanced level.[12]

New research by Jay Greene of the University of Arkansas and Josh McGee of the Arnold Foundation explodes the myth that the problem is confined to inner-city schools and minority students. In an *Education Next* article titled "When the Best is Mediocre," they compared the OECD test results with those from the National Assessment of Educational Progress (NAEP) and concluded that students in ritzy Beverly Hills, California, who are approximately 85 percent white, 7 percent Asian, 5 percent Hispanic, and 2 percent black, scored barely above average in math (53rd percentile), and those in Fairfax County, Virginia, an affluent suburb of the nation's capital, fell just below average (49th percentile).[13]

The picture is worse in big cities. Students in Washington DC stood at the 11th percentile compared with those in developed countries, in Chicago at the 21st percentile, and in New York City at the 32nd percentile. Not one of the twenty largest school districts—which enroll more than 10 percent of the nation's schoolchildren—was above the 50th percentile. Overall the results are disappointing "even in our best districts," Greene and McGee concluded. The "rare and small pockets of excellence in charter schools and rural communities are overwhelmed by large pools of failure."[14]

In a world where prosperity is almost entirely driven by brains, not brawn, we are losing the education race. We'll have to change our course dramatically if we are to have a prayer of recovering.

Learning algebra in ninth grade is not rocket science. But legions of American kids can't do it. Most public schools ask shockingly little of students. Rich, poor, or in between, our children are being permanently held back by the slipshod standards and mediocrity in our schools.

It's not just our children's futures that are at stake. As President Barack Obama has said repeatedly, "It's an economic issue when countries that out-educate us today are going to out-compete us tomorrow."[15]

THROWING MONEY AT THE PROBLEM

Let's start with a close look at how we got into this predicament. Americans have been wringing their collective hands over the shortcomings of our public education system for a half century or longer. As a country, we've repeatedly thrown money at the problem and tried reform after reform to make schools better. Presidents from Dwight D. Eisenhower (the post-Sputnik National Defense Education Act) to Lyndon B. Johnson (Head Start, Title I) to Ronald Reagan (the *A Nation At Risk* report) to George W. Bush (the No Child Left Behind Act) all made passes at the problem but came up short.

In 1989 George H. W. Bush and the nation's governors (including Bill Clinton) pledged to make American schoolkids tops in the world in math and science by 2000; that didn't happen by a long shot. George W. Bush, Senator Ted

Kennedy, and Congress decreed in 2002 that all students would be proficient in reading and math by 2014. That's not happening either.

No one can say we have not invested in education. We spend well over $10,000 a year, on average, educating each of the forty-nine million children and teens in public schools.[16] No country in the world except Luxembourg spends that much. New York State spends roughly $20,000 per pupil, double the national average. We pay teachers more than $55,000, on average, with summers off.[17] This pay is less than for other professions requiring graduate degrees, but 10 percent higher than the median household income in the United States.

Real spending (after inflation) on K–12 schools has doubled since Reagan was in the White House and quadrupled since John F. Kennedy's inauguration. (Still, it's sobering to realize that as a nation we spend almost two and a half times as much per prisoner as we do on each student.)[18]

We've expanded teaching and support staffs dramatically,[19] cutting class sizes from twenty-five-to-one to sixteen-to-one. We've made some modest gains and trimmed the shameful dropout rates in some places (including New York City), but nothing has really budged the needle. The achievement gaps between white students and minority students have narrowed somewhat on the federal government's NAEP, which is given to a cross-section of thousands of students in a variety of states each year. A third of all fourth graders and a quarter of all eighth graders have below basic reading skills; in math, 9 percent of fourth graders and 16 percent of eighth graders scored below basic. Although black and Hispanic students have made progress in the past two decades, the gulfs between majority and minority students remain monumental. In math, almost half of all black eighth graders and two-fifths of Hispanic eighth graders fall below basic compared with one-sixth of white eighth graders.[20]

Society blames poverty—Who could possibly expect black and brown kids and those from impoverished families to keep up with kids from affluent homes?—but that doesn't explain why children from privileged families are also doing poorly.

Most of the countries that are beating the pants off us—Singapore, South Korea, China, Finland, Belgium, and Canada among them—have a single education system and rigorous curriculum for all students. Singapore in particular puts us to shame. "Remember that in the early 1970s, less than half of Singapore's students even reached fourth grade. Today, Singapore ranks near the top," Secretary of Education Arne Duncan noted.[21]

We've got a crazy quilt of school districts, curricula, and standards that vary widely. Most standards are way too easy. No Child Left Behind was supposed to boost all schoolchildren to proficiency in reading and math, and to place highly qualified teachers in every classroom. Despite sharp increases in funding, the public schools have fallen far short of the lofty goals, and the U.S. Department of Education is now letting them off the hook. Although the 2002 law required every state to administer statewide tests in reading and math, it let each devise its own tests and use its own yardstick to measure results. This led to a misleading cascade of rosy test data that allowed politicians and educators to claim big progress with the same old sorry results. NAEP assessments told the real story, with a third of fourth graders reading below average and a quarter of all eighth graders scoring below basic in math.[22] The move by forty-five states to adopt the Common Core of Standards could eventually improve those scores, but that will almost certainly take years. For now we are falling behind the countries with which we compete in the international marketplace. Among the sixty-two countries plus Shanghai, Hong Kong, and Macao whose fifteen-year-olds took the OECD's Programme in International Student Assessment exams in 2009, the U.S. teens on average ranked fourteenth in reading, twenty-second in science, and twenty-ninth in math.[23] A majority of students in six countries, Shanghai, and Hong Kong were proficient in math; fewer than a third of the American fifteen-year-olds were proficient.[24]

JUST HOW LOW IS THE BAR?

Although the NAEP tests are harder than state assessments, even that bar isn't set very high. A typical question on the math test for fourth graders involves dividing a three-digit number by a one-digit number, or telling a parallel line from a perpendicular one. On reading, a third of fourth graders got this easy question wrong:

> The article says that some bees *"sparkle* in the sun." This means that these bees:
>
> 1. Like to fly in the daytime
>
> 2. Have unusual markings
>
> 3. Prefer warm weather
>
> 4. Look very shiny

Half flubbed this question, which the test writers considered to be of medium difficulty:

> The author of the story says that Willy hears only *"eerie* silence." This means that Willy:
>
> 1. Finds the silence strange and frightening
>
> 2. Believes the silence will go away soon
>
> 3. Wonders what causes the silence
>
> 4. Feels alone in the silence

The reputation of Success Academies rests in part on how well our scholars have performed on the New York State Education Department's standardized tests. We're happy and proud of their accomplishments, but also keenly aware how pathetically low the state sets its bar. Here are a couple of sample questions from New York's third-grade test:

> Sam and Jenna have been saving pennies. Sam has 232 pennies, and Jenna has 151 pennies. How many more pennies does Sam have than Jenna?
>
> 1. 71
>
> 2. 81
>
> 3. 121
>
> 4. 181
>
> Find the word or words that best complete the sentence:
> _____ came from the pillow.
>
> 1. Feathers
>
> 2. Floating
>
> 3. Soft and white
>
> 4. All over the bed

Look out, Singapore.

If you believe in equality for all, if you believe in social justice, if you believe in the American dream, the status quo in our schools is intolerable. In America, of all places, kids should not be consigned by the color of their skin or by poverty to a dropout factory. But the problem in America goes beyond tragic educational injustice. The crisis in public education affects all kids, not just our most vulnerable. Even our best schools are not putting our kids in a position to compete internationally. American children are not holding their own in what is turning out to be a fierce education race.

CHANGING KIDS' LIVES

What if it didn't have to be that way? What if poor kids, black kids, and Hispanic kids could learn as much as or more than students in most schools serving rich, white kids? And what if all American schoolchildren got a world-class education? How different would their, and our, futures be?

It sounds impossible, but that's what we're doing in Success Academies. We're doing it by rejecting the conventional wisdom that poor and minority kids cannot possibly become high achievers and that poverty and demographics are destiny.

We're fortunate to be in a position to hire the best of the best—and when they teach in Success Academies, they become even better. We are furnishing our talented principals and teachers with extraordinary amounts of time and resources to develop their craft. And when the principal and teachers are knocking the ball out of the park, the students are rounding the bases right with them. Student achievement soars, and they wind up, as our schools did, posting some of the highest scores in the city and state.

We opened our charter schools and staked our reputation on the conviction that regardless of family circumstances, children are smart and ready and eager to learn if only they have great, well-prepared principals and teachers to inspire, instruct, and direct them straight down the path to college graduation.

A HEALTHY DOSE OF COMPETITION

Why is our public school system so feeble? How did it get so bad? The late Albert Shanker, who stood up for serious reform as president of the American Federation of Teachers, once said that public schools had fallen into the same trap as the U.S. auto industry of old, thinking quality didn't matter because it had a largely captive audience for its products. More than two decades ago Shanker—who was parodied in the Woody Allen sci-fi movie *Sleeper* as a guy so militant he blew up the world—said, "It's time to admit that public education operates like a planned economy, a bureaucratic system in which everybody's role is spelled out in advance and there are few incentives for innovation and productivity. It's no surprise that our school system doesn't improve; it more resembles the communist economy than our own market economy."[25]

Well, charters came along after that to provide some badly needed competition. The common school was a good and noble thing when Horace Mann worked in the nineteenth century to create schools serving wealthy and poor alike. They educated the children of immigrants who helped make America great. They've made tremendous strides in recent decades in educating children with disabilities.

But somewhere along the line public schools got lazy and complacent, just like General Motors, Ford, and Chrysler. A lot of things came together—grade inflation, social promotion, the breakdown of discipline—and made public education a mess. Sociologist James Coleman, no stranger to controversy, roiled the waters in 1981 when he concluded after an exhaustive study that Catholic schools provided a better education for the same children than public schools.[26]

But with fewer nuns and higher costs, Catholic schools were closing left and right in our cities. Enrollment, which peaked at 5 million during the baby boom of the 1950s, stands at barely 2 million today.[27] Some states experimented with tuition tax credits and vouchers to help families pay parochial and private school tuition, but those efforts never moved beyond a small scale. A growing number of disgruntled parents turned to home schooling their children—1.5 million and growing by the National Center for Education Statistics' last count.[28]

Then charter schools emerged to give parents a new alternative and to give district schools a run for their money. Charters are public schools, often operating with less money from their city and state funders but with a lot more freedom over how the school is organized and run, from who gets hired and let go to how long students spend in class and what they study.

Charter enrollments have quadrupled over the past decade to 1.7 million, according to the Center for Education Reform, a charter advocacy organization.[29] Charters now make up 5 percent of all public schools. There are charters in forty-one states and the District of Columbia. Nine states still have laws preserving the public school monopoly: Alabama, Kentucky, Montana, Nebraska, North Dakota, South Dakota, Vermont, Washington, and West Virginia. Other states, including New York, limit the number of charters (although New York recently lifted its limit on charters from 200 to 460).

Not all charters are great. There are lousy ones, and ones that have quickly folded due to mismanagement. In some charters the students fare no better than they did back in their district school.

But then there are charters like ours that take the same kids who might founder in their neighborhood school and propel them to high achievement. As former New York City Schools' chancellor Joel Klein wrote in a June 2011 article in the *Atlantic* magazine titled "The Failure of American Schools," Success Academy Harlem 1 "now performs at the same level as the gifted-and-talented schools in New York City—all of which have demanding admissions requirements, while [Success Academy Harlem 1] randomly selects its students, mostly poor and minority, by lottery."[30]

America was built on competition. Every other sector of our society, from the auto industry to supermarkets, faces stiff competition to get better or get beaten in the marketplace by those who come along with an improved approach or product. As a nation, we face intense competition in the marketplace from China, India, and other fast-developing nations.

You can't outsource elementary and secondary education. You have to provide it locally. But people should have the right to choose what school to entrust with their child's future. The notion of competition remains anathema to the people running public schools. They resist competition at every turn, the way the U.S. Postal Service resisted FedEx when it came along.

The Postal Service went to Congress and asked that FedEx be prohibited from delivering packages. The lawmakers wisely said no, and today we've got the best, most competitive delivery system in the world. Order a replacement coffee pot or widget, and it's on your doorstep tomorrow, delivered by FedEx, UPS, or the Postal Service itself because, yes, the Postal Service after pressure to keep up with the competition has gotten much better at on-time delivery with its Express and Priority Mail.

Traditional public schools now need to face the reality that if they don't meet the competition from high-flying charters, parents are going to take their "business" elsewhere. Left to its own devices, the monopoly of district public education will never put the customer first and never find ways to boost productivity and innovate. It needs schools like ours breathing down its neck. We don't want traditional public schools to fail while charters like ours succeed; we want all schools to improve, and fast.

As Secretary Duncan said when the latest international test results came out in December 2010, "The real problem with K–12 spending in the U.S. is our low educational productivity. Unlike high-performing systems, we achieve less per dollar. And we do less to target spending on the most challenged students and schools."[31]

HIGHLY TRAINED, EXCELLENT TEACHERS MAKE THE DIFFERENCE

There's another question we need to ask ourselves: Why is it that some schools consistently deliver great results, whereas others teaching the exact same kids—from the same families, the same neighborhoods, and almost identical circumstances—never make the grade? How can one school get it right almost all the time, while one down the block (or even in the same building) almost always gets it wrong?

The short answer is that the quality of the school and the quality of the teaching both matter. With highly effective, well-trained principals and teachers, kids will soak up knowledge and ace even the toughest of tests.

Eric Hanushek, the Stanford economist who has lanced several sacred cows in education (his studies have challenged the value of cutting class size and raised doubts about the value of throwing more money at schools), has documented what a difference a great teacher can make in children's lives. In a classroom with an excellent teacher, the whole class may make a year and a half's progress in nine months. Stuck with a bad teacher in a class down the hall, similar kids may advance only half a grade level in that same school year.[32]

Same kids, different teachers, and the unlucky ones fall a year behind classmates with the great teacher. Multiply that by four years or eight years or, heaven forbid, twelve years of mediocre or worse teachers and it's no mystery why a million kids drop out of school each year. High school kids who cut school and refuse to study bear a lot of responsibility for the bind they place themselves in, but how can you blame a seven-year-old who's already a year behind in school? That child most likely is being miseducated or very, very poorly educated by a teacher and a school that just aren't doing their job. And once a child starts to fall behind, it just gets harder and harder to catch up later on.

The journalist and author Malcolm Gladwell, in his book *What the Dog Saw and Other Adventures,* summed it up: "Teacher effects dwarf school effects: your child is actually better off in a 'bad' school with an excellent teacher than in an excellent school with a bad teacher."[33] If you find a school with a great principal and lots of great teachers, it's a safe bet that the students are going to get an excellent education. Add in supportive parents, and you're on your way to success.

Charter schools don't have a monopoly on excellence. But they do have advantages that help explain why schools like ours are succeeding in places such as Harlem and the South Bronx where schools have known little but failure for years.

Charter status gives you the freedom to get things right. You don't have to play by all the rules of the school bureaucracy or abide by stifling work regulations. You have the freedom to set the school schedule and school year. You have the freedom to organize school around the best interests of children rather than the convenience of grown-ups.

We'll lay out in detail in the next chapter how we do what we do at Success Academies. But one thing we do differently than most schools is invest a tremendous amount of time and resources in training our principals and teachers and supporting their growth.

If we can do it, why can't everybody?

We think they can. The rest of this book will show you how.

CHAPTER TWO

HOW?

Making School a Magical Place

What makes for a great school? How do you deliver a world-class education to thousands of children—not children who are handpicked or sorted by test scores, but rather ordinary kids who walk through your doors?

That's the challenge we face as a nation, to figure out how to ignite learning and spur high academic achievement not just in one school or ten or a hundred, but in the thousands of public schools that educate—or miseducate—forty-nine million American students from kindergarten to twelfth grade.

Success Academies are not screened or specialized schools for the gifted and talented. We admit by random lottery, with a preference for kids living in the surrounding area and for those currently attending a failing school or whose native language is not English. Random lottery is prescribed by law in an effort to ensure that charters provide equal access and are not "boutique" schools that only those in the know or those who go to great lengths can attend. At Success Academies we actually reach out broadly, even knocking on doors, standing outside of supermarkets, and doing an extensive mail campaign to ensure that all know about the option. Last year nine thousand parents entered the random lottery for 900 spots. For the 2012–2013 school year we expect about fifteen thousand to enter the random lottery for about 1,200 spots.

So how do we do such a good job educating kids who cross our threshold through random lottery? We've done it by working incredibly hard and incredibly smart, and by giving our teachers and leaders the training and the support they need to deliver excellence in the classroom day in and day out and to push their students on to unimagined heights. We've done it with a huge assist from parents eager to do their part to stamp their child's passport to college and help him or her gain access to opportunity and the American dream.

And we've done it by transforming our schools into bright, colorful, even magical places that stir students' imagination, from the inspirational quotes on the walls to classrooms brimming with so many books they could be mistaken for the library. Every teacher has an Apple laptop and a Smart Board, an interactive whiteboard connected to the Internet. Teachers also have a tiny flip camera that plugs directly into their laptop so they can film their lessons; share them over EduTube (our own internal, YouTube-like video network); and learn from their colleagues. It's not unusual to hear Brahms or Dave Brubeck playing in the background on a CD or over Pandora while the scholars do their independent reading. Our fifth and sixth graders get Kindles.

The students don't consider themselves first graders or second graders or fourth graders. They are the Class of 2024, the Class of 2025, the Class of 2026 . . . the year they will graduate from college. That's what everyone calls them, giving the scholars a myriad of gentle reminders that they are embarked on a journey that leads to college graduation. (KIPP and other charter schools do this, too—we owe a debt of gratitude to the first generation of charter operators.) Their homeroom is not Room 318 or Room 205, but the University of Michigan or Colgate or Yale, the alma mater of their teacher. In middle school, teachers are called professors.

College isn't just in these kids' future; it's in their present.

Success Academies possess a sense of excitement and pride about learning. The pace is quick. Engagement is at a premium. The goal is to capture scholars' attention and imagination. We move at a lightning-fast clip in everything we do, from carefully practiced and planned, super-brief lessons that are limited to ten minutes, to the real-time coaching principals and leaders give teachers in the moment so they can improve their delivery even before the lesson is finished.

WOULD THEY COME IF THEY DIDN'T HAVE TO?

You don't hear a lot of repeat-after-me, drill sergeant exercises in our classrooms. We don't have a raise-your-hand culture. Our teachers do a lot of "cold calling" to get everyone involved. The scholars spend an hour and a half each day reading and discussing books, and another hour and a half writing. Of course there's math and social studies, but that's not all. We teach science every day starting in kindergarten, with five- and six-year-olds studying mealworms, dissecting squid, and doing dozens of other hands-on experiments that show them the rudiments of biology, chemistry, and even physics. It came as no surprise when New York City tested our fourth graders in science and found everyone proficient—95 percent at advanced levels! Our kids also take music, dance, arts, and sports classes and learn to play chess. We emphasize thinking in every class and every subject.

Our kids have both smarts and stamina. The scholars spend almost nine hours a day with us, arriving at 7:45 a.m. for the 8 a.m. start of classes, which last until 4:30 p.m. Some stay for an extra hour of tutoring. Kindergarten is just half an hour shorter. We almost never skip outdoor recess, even in inclement weather, because it's important for the kids to exercise their body as well as their mind. The kindergartners also get to play with blocks every day in a dedicated lab filled with blocks of multiple sizes and shapes. If you don't think blocks play a role in developing children's thinking and literacy skills, you haven't been inside one of our kindergarten labs (for more, see Chapter Five).

This curriculum is rigorous, but also interesting and lots of fun. We bring in magicians and jugglers to perform in our classrooms, adding to the sense that school is a joy, not a bore or chore. The scholars go on field trips all the time to such destinations as zoos, museums, farms, and college campuses. "We believe it's our job to make school such an interesting place for children that they can't wait to get there when they wake up every day," said Jackie Albers, principal of Success Academy Harlem 1. An important part of the jobs of our schools' leaders and teachers is making school compelling to these young scholars. Our view is that we've got to make it exciting. Here's the attitude we should take: if parents did not need child care and the kids were free not to go to school, would they come? If the answer is no, then we're not doing something right.

GOING BEYOND Z

Signs on classroom walls and in the corridors proclaim the Success Academy credo of ACTION, which stands for Agency, Curiosity, Try & Try, Integrity, Others, and No Shortcuts.

- *Agency:* Every member of our community takes ownership of ensuring that our schools are upholding the highest possible standards at everything they do.
- *Curiosity:* Our schools are fueled by wonder. Scholars ask about the world—and then use their newfound knowledge to ask more questions. Teachers immerse themselves in new ways to refine their craft.

Try & Try: We don't expect success to come easily. Our scholars and teachers understand that tackling tough challenges takes elbow grease but results in joy.

Integrity: Success Academies pride themselves on honesty and professionalism. Their members solve problems openly and quickly.

Others: We never forget to look out for each other, from offering to pitch in on a big job to simply smiling in the hallway.

No Shortcuts: Excellent learning takes time and effort. Our teachers and scholars will do what's necessary to ensure mastery of even difficult concepts.

These are not simply slogans put up on the walls; they are our deeply held philosophical beliefs and core principles. They are our religion. We exhort the children, teachers, and staff alike to go *Beyond Z,* like the imaginative character in the Dr. Seuss book *On Beyond Zebra!* who invents fantastical new letters (like *wum, fuddle,* and *vroo*) that stretch beyond the end of the conventional alphabet. There are inspirational quotes from a galaxy of inspiring figures, from Aristotle to Maya Angelou to Martin Luther King Jr. to Ray Kroc. The scholars' uniforms—plaid jumpers and orange shirts for the girls, dark slacks, blue shirts, and orange ties for the boys—mirror the schools' orange and blue colors. They wear shoes to school, not sneakers, and shirts stay tucked in. It all exudes the esprit de corps. In the hallways student art and essays are proudly displayed, along with billboards charting how many books each class and each school has read—one million books and counting in our first five years.

"A lot of little things set us apart," said Jim Manly, founding principal of Success Academy Harlem 2 and a master at the art of transforming ordinary school buildings into magical places. He's had to work this magic in two different buildings as Success Academy Harlem 2 added new grades and the city moved it from one site to the next. Not a problem; in capable hands the magic is portable.

Even the spit-and-polish bathrooms are a Success Academy trademark that stands in contrast to the messy facilities found in so many public schools. (Eva once summoned school managers to a city council hearing and demanded to know why they let bathrooms constantly run out of out of soap and toilet paper.) "All these little things make a difference in how kids view the school. They send the message that 'this is a serious place you need to respect, that we value you, and that we don't let you slip up,'" Jim said.

RIGOR AND PREPARATION

The how of Success Academies, of course, is far more than aesthetics or atmospherics. It's the rigor and breadth of the curriculum. It's the speed at which we teach. It's the care and preparation that go into every lesson, and the extraordinary amount of training and development that every principal and teacher gets on the job. They sit down as a team together at least once a week to study and practice new units. They watch film clips of themselves, colleagues down the hall, and outstanding teachers at other network schools. Classes end early on Wednesdays, and school is called off fifteen days during the year so teachers can concentrate on their professional development. In addition, leaders and new and returning teachers alike get up to four weeks of training over the summer at what we call Teacher Success Academy, or T School. All told, teachers receive the equivalent of more than thirteen weeks of training every year, and principals get eight weeks—year in and year out. This unprecedented amount of preparation is simply how we do things at Success Academies (learn more about T School in Chapter Three).

Parents are our partners in this exciting enterprise. We couldn't do it without their constant support and cooperation in helping their children reach for the stars. We are humble about what even great schools can do. They need parental support. But parental support must be cultivated. It must be encouraged and highly, highly valued and valorized. We do that at Success Academies. Our educators know what a privilege it is to have parental support. We don't take it for granted. Not a day goes by when we do not express our appreciation for sacrifices parents make for their children. Parental support makes teaching possible. Parents have the teachers' cell phone numbers and vice versa. We make frequent calls home, not only when something is amiss but also to let parents know how well their child is doing.

Under state law, we must admit students at random by lottery because the number of applications greatly exceeds the spaces available. Unfortunately, that means thousands of parents go home disappointed, although they may still have hopes that their child will get in on the wait-list or gain admission to another charter school.

The parents whose children get in feel like they have won the Powerball lottery. Their children have won tickets to college and a world-class education. The winning parents sign a compact with us, agreeing to get their scholar to school on time each morning; to read to him or her at night; to closely check and sign homework (but not to do it themselves!); to attend frequent meetings at school; and, if necessary, to come in and spend an hour on weekends at what we call Saturday Academy for children who missed work or need extra help. We have an open-door policy, so parents are welcome to come in as often as they wish and spend thirty minutes watching the instruction in their child's classroom.

We respect the children's intelligence. We know they're smart, just as smart as we are, only shorter. Even in kindergarten our teachers engage the children not in a singsong, infantilizing voice, but in elevated discourse, authentically and naturally invoking useful vocabulary that scholars need to know and emphasizing critical thinking above all else. Knowledge and know-how for us are always in support of extending our scholars' ability to interpret and understand the world as it is and as it might be.

ANATOMY FOR FIRST GRADERS

So what does this look like in action?

Take a peek inside the classroom at Success Academy Harlem 1, in which science teacher Jennifer Obiaya was teaching first graders about the similarities and differences between human and animal skeletons.

> "Humans aren't the only things that have skeletons. Put your thumb up on your lap if you can think of something else that has skeletons," said Miss Obiaya.
>
> She asked the first graders to turn to a partner and discuss the question, and told them that she would call on a scholar at random to "tell me what your partner said so I know you're being a good listener."
>
> "My partner Elijah just said a polar bear has a skeleton, too," said Yamina.
>
> "How do we know a polar bear has a skeleton? What if a polar bear didn't have a skeleton at all?" Miss Obiaya asked.
>
> "It would fall down," replied Yamina.
>
> "It would fall down, it would just be a big puddle of white fur on the ground," Miss Obiaya concurred. "What else has a skeleton?"
>
> Another child said with certainty, "My partner says a dog."
>
> "Good," said Miss Obiaya, who now projected on the Smart Board an illustration of human and dog skeletons side by side. "Wiggle your fingers if you're excited to see what we're going to do today." (We don't have a raise-your-hand-if-you-know-the-answer culture in Success Academies. Our

teachers call on everybody, ready or not. But we do encourage positive gestures like wiggling fingers, particularly in the lower grades, for scholars to show they're excited about what they are learning.)

"I need you to get into your very serious thinking pose. Do you think humans and animals have the exact same skeletons? Why or why not?" she asked. The students turned to their partner again, and, after a short, loud burst of conversations, Miss Obiaya called on Ryan.

"My partner said a dog has a tail and a cat has a tail but we don't," he said.

"Ohhhhhh!" said the teacher. "Ryan just pointed out a bone that a dog has and humans don't." A small roar of agreement went up from the scholars.

"I know it's so exciting when we make a scientific discovery like this," she said. "Today we're going to take a closer look at animal skeletons and compare—see how they are similar—and contrast—see how they are different."

She projected a new slide showing two large, overlapping circles. "When scientists compare and contrast things, Ervanni, they sometimes use a special chart like this. Tap your head if you've ever seen one of these before, maybe in writing or guided reading or maybe in science last year. Does anyone remember what this is called?" she asked.

No one came up with the answer.

"This is called a Venn diagram."

"It helps us compare and contrast how things are alike and how things are different. So in this circle we're going to write all the bones that only a human has. What do you think we're going to write in this circle? I only call on silent hands. Ciyann?"

"Umm, only animals."

"Right, only bones that in this case dogs have. What do you think goes in the middle circle, Shari, if these are things only humans have, and these are things only dogs have?"

Softly Shari answered, "The things that dogs and humans have?"

"Yessss," said Miss Obiaya with gusto, "the things that both humans and dogs have. Fantastic. Who wants to help me out?" She called on the students to think of bones to place in the Venn diagram. (It was quite a lesson for six-year-olds, and this is what they were getting every day in Miss Obiaya's class.)

On another morning with the same kids, the teacher asked the students to "make a hypothesis, a smart guess," about whether caterpillars would prefer a smooth surface or a rough one in their habitat.

"I think the caterpillar will go to rough because when I was in kindergarten, I was in your class. All the caterpillars . . ." said Katy.

"All the earthworms," Miss Obiaya reminded her.

"All the earthworms went to rough."

"Wow, what I love about Katy's hypothesis is she didn't just say, 'I think the caterpillars will go to rough.' She said, 'I think the caterpillar will go to rough BECAUSE . . .' and then she gave a reason," the teacher said. If anyone doubts whether science lessons in kindergarten stick, Katy's answer is proof otherwise.

Most public schools in New York City don't teach science daily until middle school. The situation is the same in elementary schools across the country. To us, that boggles the mind. If our kids don't have a solid grounding in science and math, how can they possibly compete against the hard-charging graduates of schools in the countries that are our economic rivals? An elementary school without daily, discovery-oriented science and dedicated science teachers isn't doing its job.

Science teaches children more than the basic laws of gravity and the different types of species. It capitalizes on their natural curiosity. It teaches them to think clearly and to make arguments based on evidence and sound reasoning. It expands their vocabulary and enhances valuable reading and math skills, including the ability to understand charts, graphs, and data. Does anybody think the schools in Singapore, Japan, China, or India are waiting that long to teach science? This has to change, and we're doing our part in Success Academies. We're banking on the fact that teaching kids to make scientific hypotheses in kindergarten will get them ready to excel in chemistry and physics in high school and then to major in the sciences at the best colleges.

LETTING CHILDREN DO THE THINKING WORK

Our scholars read all the time, including for long, uninterrupted stretches in class every day. We also devote large blocks of time to writing, because we are convinced that you become a great reader by reading voluminously and a great writer by writing up a storm. It surprises some visitors to Success Academies that in a ninety-minute reading class, the teacher's lesson at the front of the room may last no more than ten minutes, with the rest of the period devoted to independent reading and coaching students in small groups to tackle the thesis or major theme of a book that would be hard for the children to read independently. Even in kindergarten the whole class will have extended conversations about the books they read. The teacher often reads them a book above their grade level and sparks a debate about the book. The scholars are as young as five, but when these book discussions get cooking they can be as absorbing and insightful as a college literature seminar. The teacher has studied the book intently beforehand. Dr. Seuss isn't William Faulkner, but there is more depth and more to ponder in great works of children's literature than many adults remember or have ever recognized at all.

Our teachers know better than to hand the scholars these insights on a silver platter. By knowing the book backward and forward, and by preparing penetrating questions ahead of time, they are able to spark a great discussion while still allowing the scholars to do the critical thinking work. Whether they are reading an Aesop's fable or a Tomie DePaola book, we want them to think deeply about and discuss the meaning of what they are reading. We also want them to evaluate their interpretations and find the parallels between what they read and their own young lives.

Candido Brown, an inspiring founding first-grade teacher at Success Academy Harlem 2 and now a fourth-grade teacher there, got a reminder about this one morning while we observed his Harvard classroom with the school's principal, Jim Manly. Mr. Brown was presiding over a class discussion of *The Name Jar,* a book by Yangon Choy about a Korean-American girl who faces pressures from classmates to adopt an American name. Mr. Brown waxed impatient for his scholars to grasp the full import of the book's message.

When one of Mr. Brown's students said Unhei (literally "grace" in Korean) should keep her name because "it means you're a good person," the teacher interjected, "Let me just jump in a little bit. It's not just about your name, it's about your ___" He left a pregnant pause and waited for students to fill in the blank. "It's about *your* ___" he repeated. After several stabs, a girl came up with the word Mr. Brown was looking for: "culture."

"It's about your *culture,*" the teacher said with gusto, "it's about your culture, right? Her *name* ___"

"Stop, Mr. Brown," interjected Mr. Manly. "Let's see if they can finish, because you're about to tell them. Let them tell us. Why is your culture so important? Think about that, scholars. Go." The first graders picked up the ball, and the conversation took off, with only occasional interjections by the teacher. The kids even called on one another to speak.

The principal's timely, brief intercession did the job. It worked in real time. The students, not their teacher, carried the conversation. Afterward, outside the class, Mr. Manly said he saw a lot of himself as a novice teacher in Mr. Brown. "He teaches like I taught. I fell in love with the sound of my own voice. He was so full of ideas and enthusiasm, he couldn't wait for the scholars to get it for themselves," the principal said. The lesson wasn't lost on Mr. Brown, who later in the day vowed, "From now on, I'm going to talk less. I need to keep my mouth shut."

Mr. Brown, already a wonderful teacher just three years into his career, is an educator who soaks up every ounce of professional development and asks for more. "I love it. I beg Jim, I beg all the leadership residents: 'If you see something I could do to improve my practice, tell me right in the moment. Don't send me an e-mail later. Then it's too late. Give it to me now.'" He added, "I'm not afraid of feedback. It helps me tremendously. It moves my practice. That's what I thrive on."

AN ENGLISH LITERATURE SEMINAR FOR FIVE-YEAR-OLDS

The trademarks of THINK Literacy are the stimulating book talks that take place every day, even in kindergarten and first-grade classrooms. Take for instance the discussion that Success Academy Bronx 1 kindergarten teacher Jennifer Haynes orchestrated with her scholars about *Tico and the Golden Wings* by Leo Lionni, a book about a wingless little bird ostracized by friends after he magically gets a pair of golden wings. Ms. Haynes read the story aloud to her class of twenty-eight, stopping frequently to do think alouds in which she modeled asking herself the kinds of questions that a good reader asks with any piece of literature.

 Clip 2   Read Aloud, Kindergarten

In this video we see that in Ms. Haynes's kindergarten classroom at Success Academy Bronx 1, read aloud time means anything *but* your typical bedtime story. Rather, Ms. Haynes uses every second to envelope her scholars in the magic of a great book, and to teach her kindergartners the kind of thinking great readers do.

How does she do this?

Ms. Haynes **has intellectually prepared at a high level**. She has read *Tico and the Golden Wings* several times in order to pull out key ideas and evidence to support them. She has planned strategic stopping points, both to *think aloud,* letting kids in on her own ideas, and for scholars to *turn and talk* about important parts of the book. Ms. Haynes's deep understanding both of the purpose of a read aloud and of the book **sets her scholars up for success** as they work to understand the book's meaning.

Ms. Haynes also understands that although *short,* her five-year-olds are enormously capable of thinking critically and supporting their ideas with evidence from the book. So she **aims high** and **talks to kids like they're smart.** She doesn't exhaust herself or infantilize her scholars by using a slow, singsong voice! Instead, she addresses her kindergartners as fellow readers and thinkers, using normal adult vocabulary to talk about the book. The result? Ms. Haynes's scholars feel like they've been invited into an adult book club, and they rise to clear the high bar their teacher has set.

Ms. Haynes finished reading *Tico and the Golden Wings* and had the students rearrange themselves around the perimeter of the rug for the freewheeling book discussion. The plot is one that children everywhere can relate to. The other birds had been kind to Tico when he couldn't fly, but they turn on him when he wakes up one day with gleaming golden wings. Tico flies off around the world, eventually giving away his prized golden feathers to people in need. Real feathers grow back to replace them, and when Tico arrives back home he gets a warm welcome from the others, now all birds of the same feather.

"What lesson did Tico learn?" Ms. Haynes asked. The children wrestled with what message to take from Leo Lionni's story.

"His friends just needed him to look like them because they think he wanted to be better than them," said Aden, "but he just wanted to be like the other birds."

Hunter agreed, saying Tico gave away the golden wings so "his friends would like him and stop saying the bad things."

"I think that even though you are different from your friends, you can still be friends," said Ashley.

"Ashley, that makes me think of the last line of the book," said Ms. Haynes. Opening to that page, she read, "His friends say, 'Now you're just like us,' but Tico says, 'Now my wings are black, but I am not like my friends. We are all different for each has his own memories and his own invisible, golden dreams.'" That sparked further discussion of Tico's motivation, his desire to fit in, and yet his recognition of the need to be himself. Two children brought up the similarities between this book and another the class had read called *The Rainbow Fish* by Marcus Pfister, in which the main character gives up his iridescent scales.

Clip 3 — Book Discussion, Kindergarten

As you watch this video, notice the degree to which the kindergartners own and carry the conversation. In this clip, it's evident that Ms. Haynes has taught her scholars exactly what it means to **actively listen** during a discussion, and to participate fully in one's own learning. Her scholars know that to learn they must speak audibly, follow the speaker with their eyes, ask for clarification when they don't understand, and respond to each other's ideas.

Ms. Haynes also gets sky-high levels of scholar ownership of the conversation by **letting the kids do the thinking work.** She lets her scholars grapple with the question of whether Tico gave the golden feathers away simply to help others or to gain acceptance from his friends. Ms. Haynes knows that letting kids do the intellectual heavy lifting will keep them on the edge of their seat (or rug spot). Ms. Haynes has done her own intellectual heavy lifting by studying the book prior to the lesson, so she is ready to join the conversation at strategic points, drawing scholars' attention to excerpts from the book that will drive the conversation forward.

It was a lot for five- and six-year-olds to take from a short picture book, and it happened because the teacher laid the groundwork for a great discussion and came prepared with good questions. Looking back on the conversation,

Ms. Haynes said, "It's very important to let them continue to do the thinking work even if they struggle, because if you never struggle, you never move past that point."

This is what we aim for in every book discussion. Feeding children the answers or saving them from intellectual struggle is not educating them. Kids need to learn how to think a problem through. At Success Academies we teach teachers to ask great questions about books and resist giving kids the answers. Students should work through questions together. Classmates demand evidence and challenge their friends. The discussion gets richer, and the learning is far more powerful. This is how we teach students to read and interpret books, poems, and other pieces of writing.

DISCOVERING MEANING

The book talks sparkled as well in Andrea Klein's fourth-grade class at Success Academy Harlem 1. Mrs. Klein, who now works with teachers across the network as one of our in-house literacy experts, read aloud Chris Van Allsburg's *The Wretched Stone,* a story about a mysterious, glowing stone that mesmerizes sailors who bring it back to their ship and eventually turns them into apes. The spell is only broken when the ship's captain helps the crew rediscover their love of music and storytelling. First sitting with a small group of students, the teacher asked, "What has caused this transformation in the crew? What has caused them to change from sailors to apes?"

"The stone. It has this type of power, and it's drawing them in," said Cherish.

"Maybe they got drawn in by the light, which made them very lazy," said Geneva.

"So they changed," said Mrs. Klein.

"They changed from being sailors that enjoyed music and dancing and stories . . . into lazy apes," replied Damon.

"There's some sort of trance almost that they seem to be in. Is there something like that in your life?" the teacher asked.

"The TV," Cherish said with a knowing smile as she outlined the familiar box with her fingers. Television, according to Cherish, has the power to make adults and children "really lazy, just sitting there all day doing nothing but watching the TV."

Now, these scholars probably did not go home and ask their parents to permanently unplug the family television, but we bet the message of *The Wretched Stone* will stay with them for a long, long time.

Clip 4   **Book Discussion, Third Grade**

In this video Mrs. Klein, who now works with teachers across our network and is one of our in-house literacy experts, is **intellectually prepared at a high level.** Mrs. Klein facilitates the book discussion with a road map of questions that build toward the main idea of the book. **Having this road map prepared in advance allows Mrs. Klein to listen closely to kids.** (Notice how she takes notes as they share their ideas.) In her planning, Mrs. Klein has determined exactly what it will sound like when she closes the deal and kids understand the book at the deepest level. Having this end goal in mind allows her to constantly drive toward it.

BREAKTHROUGHS WITH THE ADULTS

For us, it's gospel that the adults hold the key to high achievement in Success Academies. Kids will do extraordinary things and defy expectations if they attend schools that are efficiently run, serious, and staffed by talented, well-trained principals and teachers who aren't beholden to the conventional wisdom of what "poor" kids can do and learn.

But it's not just a matter of attitude and beliefs.

Our teachers and leaders get amazing results because they work extremely hard and extremely smart, and because they get help and opportunities to grow every day on the job. "What I tell my staff is, 'You have the right to be professionally developed. Each day you should feel that you go home a better teacher than when you came in this morning,'" said Vanessa Bangser, principal of Success Academy Bronx 2. "It's our job as school leaders to make that happen."

We believe it's hypocritical to expect the children to learn and grow by leaps and bounds while not expecting the adults to grow and expand their repertoire just as much and just as fast. And this is something that teachers crave, as shown by the fact that we receive tons of applications for every opening in our classrooms (57,000 teacher resumes for the 256 spots for the 2011–2012 school year!). We don't hire teachers by lottery, as we do the scholars. Instead we look for the best and brightest and for those who are eager and hungry for feedback. We get veterans who crave the coaching that is almost totally absent from their old schools and new teachers hungry to learn.

We'll explain more in the next chapter about our fixation with adults. What we know is that it helps us get great results.

PARTNERSHIP WITH PARENTS

No matter how talented the teachers or how strong the curriculum, no school can run on all cylinders without wholehearted support and involvement from parents. Our parents sign on to do their part at home when they enroll their child in a Success Academy. Unfortunately, because space is limited, they must enter a lottery to get their child in, but we are expanding and opening new schools as fast as possible to meet the demand. We'd much rather accommodate everyone or operate in a system in which parents have lots of good choices of which school to have their child attend. We agree with Bill Gates, the Microsoft founder and philanthropist, when he said, "There is already enough in life that depends on luck. When it comes to education, we should replace luck with equity."[1]

Along with the claim that poverty makes it nearly impossible for children to learn at high levels in most inner-city schools, you often hear the assertion that the parents of these children aren't that interested in their education and are hard to get involved in the life of the school, whether it's attending back-to-school night or coming to meetings with the classroom teacher. Our experience is the opposite. Success Academy parents are intensely interested in their child's education and determined, as we are, that their son or daughter will be marching across that college stage in 2022 (our oldest class) and beyond. They know the difference between a good school and a lousy school. They also know almost unerringly who the very best teachers are, and they want their child in those classes. The problem is one of supply, NOT demand. We have found that the mama- or papa-bear instinct transcends class, race, and ethnicity. Parents want their kid to have a better life than they themselves had, and they try their best to provide that for their child.

As we noted earlier, our parents sign a symbolic compact with us that requires them to read at home to their child, to monitor homework, and to stay in close contact with the classroom teacher and the school. All of our principals, teachers, and staff give out business cards with their cell phone numbers on them, and the teachers and the front office have the parents' phone numbers as well. The parents have been our first and foremost partners. We wouldn't be here with nine schools today if parents had not sacrificed, making sure the homework was done, bringing kids in early, staying late, coming to Saturday Academy, and making all the regular sacrifices. One of our most active parents, Genevieve Foster, whose daughter Geneva started in kindergarten at Success Academy Harlem 1 in

2007 and is now a fourth grader, describes the partnership between parents and teachers as "a marriage of sorts." Parents such as Genevieve have stood beside network leaders, teachers, and staff at countless hearings in which New York City Schools panels were making decisions about the fate of our academies and other charters. They rallied behind us when the local teachers union and the New York branch of the NAACP went to court to block our newest schools. They lost their lawsuit, and the civil rights group was excoriated by newspaper editorial boards for standing in the way of greater educational opportunity for minority students. Genevieve said Success Academy parents won't back down. "You need to know as parents we are going to stand beside you and back you up 110 percent. You have parents who are serious about expressing their right to choose what school is best for their children. We need to fight this battle together. These children are going to be our presidents, our doctors, our lawyers. We are absolutely not going anywhere. We'll be here for a long time to come."

We don't ask our parents to bake brownies or sell wrapping paper for their school. We want something more important. The *Success Academy Family Handbook* makes this clear: "We know that scholars need to excel at high levels given the global competition. We want to do whatever it takes to equip your scholar to graduate from college, but we cannot be successful without your support."

One frigid February night dozens of parents turned out for a hearing in Brooklyn in which the city's Panel for Educational Policy was deciding the fate of several of our schools. They left work early, had relatives mind their children or brought the children with them, and came all the way from Harlem and the Bronx over the Manhattan Bridge to Brooklyn. They then walked the final blocks over snow-covered streets to the marathon hearing in Brooklyn Tech's cavernous auditorium. They were impossible to miss in their orange Success Academy T-shirts.

On the way down to the hearing, Aicha Katen, an immigrant from Guinea in West Africa and mother of a first grader, said, "I left my job early to come because I want to fight for my kids. I want my kids to learn more." She added, "If you show them how to learn, one day they're going to say, 'Oh, yes, my parents, they fight for me to learn something.'"

Ayisha Winslow said her second-grade son was thriving at Success Academy Harlem 2. "He wants to go to college. That's one thing about Harlem Success I love, the fact that they show the kids that it's more than just kindergarten through eighth grade . . . They push them to see that it's beyond that: college and getting a good job, financial security and a career," said Ayisha, a high school dropout now working on getting her GED. "Basically, when I look over his homework and stuff, it's all like a learning experience for me," she said. "We all can learn together."

Maleeka Knight's son won a space in first grade after attending kindergarten elsewhere. "It's a huge difference. There is more structure, more discipline. Last year in kindergarten he was extremely bored. Now he's stimulated," said Maleeka.

With parents like these as partners, it's no wonder that the young scholars are doing great things and are poised to accomplish even more.

That is how we do it at Success Academies: we embrace rigorous, world-class standards and teach with passion. We focus on helping the adults improve their performance, knowing that big gains for the children will follow automatically. We engage the parents as essential partners. It's a formula we're convinced can work for other schools, too, regular or charter.

TAKEAWAYS

Here's what you can do to make your school a place where the magic of learning happens every day in every classroom. It starts not with the children, but with the adults—principals, teachers, parents, and school reformers.

PRINCIPALS: Give teachers the time and training they need to up their game, and big gains in student achievement will follow. And raise the bar.

TEACHERS: Believe in your students and believe in your own ability to master content. Make joyful rigor your mantra. Work with colleagues to practice and perfect lessons. Seek help from your principal and other leaders. Don't doubt that the kids will get it if you consistently make the instruction both challenging AND interesting.

PARENTS: The teachers can't do it by themselves. They need you pushing as well to help students keep charging ahead and get ready for college. Visit your child's classroom, talk with the teacher about what you can do at home to speed the learning, and stand up for world-class schooling. Without parents demanding a world-class education, we won't have it in our schools.

SCHOOL REFORMERS: Recognize how deep a hole our schools are in and admit that the problems aren't confined to inner-city schools or students growing up in poverty. Don't get distracted by debates over class size or other side issues, and don't be fooled by state exams that purportedly show every child as being above average. The real test is how American kids stack up against the rest of the world. The problem is not one of the urban poor, it is a national one. We must marshal forces to win the future. Winning will entail making schools magical, compelling places that place a premium on rigor and engagement.

CHAPTER THREE

WHO?

It's All About the Adults

We'll say it again.

It's all about the adults.

This simple but profound idea is totally radical and at odds with almost every other approach that's been tried to fix America's schools. It's the basis, however, for everything we do at Success Academies, where we're showing that with world-class teaching, kids from distressed communities like Harlem and the South Bronx can compete with and even outperform children from New York City's wealthiest zip codes. We've expanded our network of schools now to Manhattan's Upper West Side and to Brooklyn because families there are also hungry for great schools.

Achieving excellence isn't about the students. It's about the grown-ups. When the grown-ups are running on all cylinders, they bring the kids along for the swift, exhilarating ride. There have always been isolated schools with inspiring teachers who help youngsters beat the odds in difficult circumstances. We're doing it in every Success Academy with hard work, study, perspiration, and inspiration by the adults.

It's not just that the teachers are setting an example for the scholars—which they are—but also that they become so skilled at sharing that knowledge and mastery that their students can surmount serious disadvantages and prepare themselves to compete with the best students in the world. It begins with the incredible amount of time, preparation, coaching, and resources our principals and teachers get to make the absolute most of their day. We believe it's simply hypocritical to expect the children to learn and grow rapidly without demanding that we adults learn and improve our abilities just as fast.

We ask and expect a lot of our teachers and principals, but they also get more support and undergo more development than any educators in New York City—and, as far as we know, anywhere in the country.

"I've never been in a school where the adults are concentrated on so much and where our development is considered so important," said Danique Loving, the principal of Success Academy Harlem 4, a mother of three, and a classroom veteran with fifteen years' teaching experience. "This is what's unique about us: we know that the kids can't go to where they need to go and do the things they need to achieve at high levels if the adults can't take them there."

Kelsey Contreras, formerly one of our kindergarten teachers at Success Academy Harlem 1 and now on the network literacy team, began her career teaching in the South Bronx. "I felt I was in the trenches. There wasn't a lot of support. It was kind of like everyone was in their own classroom doing their own thing," she recalled. Colleagues were trying hard, "but it wasn't organized in a way to help teachers who were starting out." At Success Academy Harlem 1, "everyone was on the same page, everyone was working their hearts out and the administration was on board." She craved the constructive criticism that Success Academy leaders were constantly providing. Watching videotaped lessons together reminded her of being back in high school, where she competed on the dance team and after every competition watched videos of her performance. She was her own toughest critic. "I'd rewind and replay them and say, 'My toe's not pointed here; I need to fix it.' That's what this is like here. We'll watch a video, and they'll give me feedback. It helps me be a better teacher. Each year I got so much better," she said.

The demand from parents for space in our free, public charter schools is extraordinary, as was documented in the movies *Waiting for Superman* and *The Lottery*. But so is the interest from aspiring and experienced teachers alike who want to come teach in Success Academies and learn how we do it. Tens of thousands apply every year to teach and to lead at our schools. "Why? It's because of the unprecedented level of training and support we offer teachers," said Jackie Albers, principal of Success Academy Harlem 1. They're flocking to Success Academies to be part of a revolution that is shattering old beliefs about what's possible in big city schools serving mostly poor and minority students and also what's possible across the board.

Teachers in particular are interested in commonsense solutions that make a material impact on student learning. When they are confident and well prepared, their students learn at higher levels. In some ways, it's that simple. So at Success Academies we invest heavily in the adults. Educators are our most precious resource, and we treat them that way, constantly helping them learn the art and science of teaching. Our teachers find that this laser-like focus on teaching in their classroom improves student learning dramatically day after day. They report that their children's progress is inspiring and even mind-blowing.

But it's also extremely hard work. Like in the gym, no pain, no gain. The experienced teachers we hire, like Danique, were accustomed to being stars where they used to teach, with their youngsters showing the way for everyone else. "What I tell [applicants] all the time is, 'If you come here, be prepared to be in a network of superstars. Everyone that we hire was the top performer at their old school,'" said Danique. Some are crestfallen to quickly discover here at Success Academies that teachers down the hall—all teaching the same lessons to students with the same range of abilities—are moving their kids faster. "They say, 'Wait a minute. *I* used to be the one with the best lesson plans or bulletin boards or ideas.' All of a sudden you're in a group of highflyers and high achievers, and it can be a shock," Danique said.

But with great coaching and teamwork, new teachers can quickly make that adjustment. Our teachers never feel marooned in the classroom. There's a second roaming teacher in the room to help during most reading, writing, and math lessons. We call them associate teachers. Many are new to the profession, but they would be assigned to a class by themselves in most public schools. We can do this because we elect to have larger class sizes—typically twenty-eight students, sometimes thirty—and redirect the savings into hiring more teachers.

There's also no danger that our teachers and their scholars will drop off the radar and fall so far behind that it's hard to catch up. Principals and their assistants, called leadership residents, make the rounds of classrooms every day, watching the instruction and coaching the teachers right then and there on how to improve their delivery. We also make frequent rounds of Success Academies to join the principal and leaders on these speed observations of THINK Literacy lessons. A kindergarten teacher may have the network CEO in his or her class five or six times during the course of the year, and see the principal ten times that often.

What a contrast with most public schools.

Carrie Roby, a phenomenal second-grade math teacher, then leadership resident, and now principal of Success Academy Upper West, recalled, "At my old school in the South Bronx the principal literally came into my room once a year. I knew I was not perfect. I knew I could do it better. I was doing all the things I knew how to do to improve, but at a certain point you need somebody else who has more experience, another eye to come in. People here are looking for that."

For second-grade teacher Dionne Beckford, it was a similar story. She began her teaching career after graduating from the University of Pennsylvania (also Eva's alma mater) back at the same struggling public elementary school that she had attended growing up in Stamford, Connecticut. There "they give you the curriculum, they give you the manuals, and it's 'All right, have at it,'" said Dionne. "You might see a leader come into your room three times out of the whole year, or maybe never if you're a good teacher because they figure you're OK. If the parents don't complain, they pretty much leave you alone."

"In a lot of schools, teachers languish; it's OK to be mediocre. That's what I love the most here, that you're being held accountable. Someone comes in and says, 'OK, here's what I noticed. Here are some next steps to improve your practice.' Teachers are on their toes," said Dionne, now a leadership resident at Success Academy Harlem 2.

Teachers come to us knowing that they are going to get at least two and sometimes three periods a day to prepare and practice lessons, working with the other teachers of the same grade and practicing as well with the school's leadership team. The principal is unquestionably the school's instructional leader, freed from administrative chores and distractions by the existence of a separate building manager, who is responsible for finances, procurement, the maintenance and aesthetics of the building, and all of the other noninstructional responsibilities that district principals must shoulder. The network office also handles administrative burdens, such as sourcing teacher candidates, administering staff benefits, preparing and analyzing data, and recruiting students, that might otherwise fall to a principal working for a traditional school district.

The assistant principals, or those we call leadership residents (like doctors in residence who are learning the craft), devote most of their time and energy to helping the teachers prepare lessons and coaching them in the classroom. It helps us all move forward in unison because the same lessons are taught on the same day across the same grades, not only in that one school but across the network. Sometimes we'll have a highflyer teach the lesson a day or two early, film it, and share it with colleagues of that grade via our own EduTube network.

Clip 5   **Prepared Versus Not Prepared**

So often teachers suffer from what we call *misplaced preparation*. They've stayed up late, they've made the elaborate charts, they've even laminated. **And yet, despite all of their efforts, the lesson tanks.** The issue, of course, is not that the teacher hasn't worked incredibly hard, but rather that he or she hasn't "worked smart." **To work smart, teachers must invest in doing the intellectual preparation, NOT in bells and whistles.** In contrast to the first segment of this clip, the second segment shows a confident teacher who understands that the purpose of direct reading instruction is to teach kids one aspect of great reading that will transfer into their independent practice. She has invested in understanding *why* her teaching point is useful (in this case because the fun of reading a mystery is to solve the mystery *before* the sleuth) and picked strategic spots in the book both to model this point and to have kids experience its utility. Watch these segments again and **check the kids' faces for understanding.** As you do, you will see a marked difference between the first and second segments, based on the teacher's level of intellectual preparation.

The constant focus at Success Academies on watching teaching and the emphasis on continuous improvement are attractions, not drawbacks, for those who want to be great teachers. "It's not a surprise to people that we hire. We know who we are. This is the philosophy of adult learning, the sense of constant improvement. You're always going to get next steps, no matter what," said Vanessa Bangser, the principal of Success Academy Bronx 2. "It's not [that] you're not good enough. It's about making you better out of profound respect for you as a professional . . . You should go home each day feeling that you're a better teacher than you were this morning."

Arin sent that message loud and clear to our new hires at the summer training and orientation program we call Teacher Success Academy, or T School: "If you don't get direct feedback, demand it. If you were paying for a personal trainer and they worked you out for an hour and didn't give you any tips, you'd feel ripped off. That's how you should feel if your leader isn't constantly helping you step up your game."

A TALE OF TWO CLASSROOMS

There are basically two approaches that principals can take when they enter a classroom and spot things that are amiss. The first approach is to step in and start fixing the problems out loud, one by one—calling out students by name and telling them to quit talking, or get their book out and start reading, or stop sharpening their pencil. This is what happens in most schools. We take the opposite approach. Our principal walks in, quickly assesses the situation, and immediately heads to the teacher and works with her or him, not with the kids.

Here's how these two scenarios might play out in the same classroom.

SCENARIO ONE: FIXING KIDS

The principal walks into a second-grade class during independent reading. Most of the twenty-eight students are reading silently at their desk while the teacher circulates among them, offering words of encouragement and helping students who are stuck on a hard passage. It's easy to have tunnel vision while doing this and, unless it happens right under her nose, the teacher may overlook and ignore the half-dozen students who either aren't reading at all or are just going through the motions. Some may not even have opened the book or, if it is open, aren't turning pages, or they're flipping through them faster than speed readers. If the noise level gets too high, the teacher will glance up and tell the class to quiet down, but mainly she is bent on making her rounds, focusing on one kid at a time.

*The principal can see at a glance who is not working. He pounces on the ringleaders. "Keyshawn, sit up straight. Natalia, focus on your book. Ethan, turn your chair around. Isaiah, what page are you supposed to be reading?" In the space of fifteen seconds the principal has corralled all the stragglers, the distracted, and the dillydalliers and got their noses back in their books, at least for now. As soon as the principal exits, half these kids revert to wasting time, while the other half continue reading. The teacher now is worried and flustered. What had she missed that was so obvious to the principal? Exactly what had the principal done? Is she in trouble? She remains in the dark about how to keep all twenty-eight scholars on task during independent reading. **Result: The leader focused on the kids. The teacher is no more effective than before. Student outcomes are unchanged.***

SCENARIO TWO: INVESTING IN THE ADULTS

The principal walks into the classroom during independent reading and can see at a glance what's going wrong. For an experienced eye, students who aren't really reading are easy to spot. The principal withstands the temptation to march over and straighten each one out, and instead makes a beeline for the teacher. Sotto voce, he points out the students who require immediate attention. "Natalia is flipping through the pages; she's not really reading. Keyshawn has been on the same page for three minutes; he's not reading, he's faking it. Cecilia is glancing at one book for forty-five seconds, then rummaging through her backpack to pull out a new one."

With the teacher in tow, the principal now moves alongside two of these students, modeling how to get them back on the beam. A few words suffice. Then it's the teacher's turn. The principal watches while she quickly reels in two more wayward scholars. The rest get the message and start reading before they are spoken to. In short order the entire class is immersed in books. The principal moves on to the next class, where again, after a quick assessment, he points out the problems to the teacher and coaches him on how to set things straight.

Problems like this are rarely unique to one classroom, so the principal follows up with an e-mail to the entire grade-level team that afternoon reminding them how important independent reading is for all students and what to keep an eye out for. The principal suggests three next steps or ways to improve the quality of independent reading, which lasts up to forty-five minutes each day. And the very next morning the principal is back during independent reading to make sure the teachers have taken the advice. **Result: The leader focused on the adults. Teachers' efficacy improved rapidly. The results are reflected in better student outcomes.**

CYCLE OF TEACHER IMPROVEMENT

Our leaders follow a regular, six-step routine for helping teachers become masters of their craft. This is what we call the Cycle of Teacher Improvement:

Step One: Speed Observations (Round One)

Leaders—principals and leadership residents or members of the literacy team—conduct speed observations in every classroom on the same grade on the same morning. These are a series of rapid, back-to-back observations lasting no more than five to ten minutes each. Because all the teachers on the grade team are teaching the same lesson, leaders can quickly spot the differences. This itself requires training. Principals need to develop a keen eye for what to look for. But once trained, principals can quickly determine through their observations what kinds of problems they have on their hands. At worst, observations are used as a compliance tool for supervisors to rate their teachers twice a year. At best, observations are used to tell teachers afterward what principals have observed. For Success Academies, speed observations are a tool that principals use to immediately diagnose problems and suggest solutions and to notice what needs fixing or is working exceedingly well so they can spread the word.

Step Two: Study Groups

The school leader or leadership resident (the principal or assistant principal, respectively, in a traditional school) calls the teachers together for a study group to share what he or she observed in the various classrooms and discuss how to prepare for and teach this lesson and the ones that follow more effectively. They may watch a video of the lesson being taught at a high level by a colleague or a teacher at another school in the network. The leader also may model how to teach this lesson or another one. (Study groups take place during the day when the students are in science, art, music, or classes other than reading, writing, and math, or on Wednesday afternoons when all classes end at 2:00 p.m. and a three-hour period is set aside for professional development.) The theory here is that the content matters. Teaching is not merely a series of procedures. For effective teaching to occur, principals must study and understand the curriculum, and they must become highly effective at teaching their teachers to study the content. They must also think through what students will miss or struggle with and how to present the material in an engaging way. There is no substitute for studying. This lost art form must be brought back. Without it, we cannot improve teacher practice.

Step Three: Teachbacks

The study group participants take turns teaching a portion of the lesson to each other. They do it in quick succession, each person getting clear, direct feedback after his or her turn from the principal and peers. We call these teachbacks. No children are present, but it's a dress rehearsal for what each teacher will do in front of kids. The theory here is that teaching is at once a highly intellectual activity involving understanding complex material as well as a craft, a practice. To become a great teacher, you have to practice and practice again . . . and sometimes again and again. This step is skipped only at kids' peril.

Step Four: Labsites

Teachbacks are followed by labsites. We call them labsites because teachers go into an actual classroom and practice teaching actual kids while being coached by the principal, who moves rapidly from one teacher's group of students to the next. In a class with thirty kids, groups of six teachers, each with five children, make up the labsite. The principal can quickly make the rounds, coaching all six teachers in each group and helping them up their game in real time. Afterward the principal and the teachers reconvene to discuss what worked best and what they would do differently the next time. The theory of labsites is that although practicing in front of your peers is helpful (and perhaps initially safer), the real test only comes when you're doing it in the classroom with children. You can diagram football and basketball plays all you want in the locker room and then practice them on the field, but eventually you have to put them to the test in a real game. There are no shortcuts. To move student learning forward, teachers must practice with kids, and principals must practice with teachers. And it takes an awful lot of practice to make good, let alone perfect.

Step Five: Speed Observations (Round 2)

The leader returns to the same teachers' classrooms the next day to find out if the rehearsal session has in fact moved teacher practice to a higher level. The principal or leader figures out not only what worked but also how to push the teacher improvement cycle further to obtain even bigger gains and improvements in teacher practice. Based on these quick observations, the principal plans additional study and practice sessions.

Step Six: Individual Coaching

The leader follows up with individual support and coaching as needed, giving the teachers immediate feedback while the lesson is under way, sitting down with them afterward, or both. Because the principal's time is limited, we like to start with challenges that are germane to all teachers. But differentiation is ultimately necessary because the teachers often are at different levels of their practice. A one-size-fits-all model of development does not do justice to the varied needs that teachers have. That's where the individual coaching comes in. A principal actually may start by trying to move the top teachers from good to great. That takes less time than working with those who have the most ground to make up. And the principal then has the example of the high-flying teachers to help with the rest. Leveraging our internal teaching talent is a critical part of our model at Success Academies. It all rests on the principals' coaching the teachers to move their practice *Beyond Z*.

LEADER STUDY GROUPS

Our principals and other leaders—including the authors—also are learning on the job, and we don't leave that to happenstance, either. Principals engage in their own, regular forms of professional development, studying and practicing together to sharpen their understanding of what we teach, how we teach, and why we teach it. Frequently, before meeting with their teachers to prepare to launch into a new THINK Literacy unit, principals spend several hours practicing and game-planning the lessons themselves in what we call a Leader Study Group. Every other week they put aside all other school business for a full morning and converge on one of the Success Academies for a Leader Study Group, during which they study and plan lessons together, practice on each other and sometimes with the teachers and children in that school, and map out coaching and intervention strategies to bring back to their own Success Academy. They figure out what we call "premortems," which are all the things we can think of that can possibly go wrong in the classroom while the lesson is actually taught. Everyone understands what postmortems are. Good, well-thought-out premortems can spare everyone the need to conduct a postmortem when something goes awry. The premortems are not about mistakes the students are likely to make. They're about the things the adults in the classroom are likely to mess up. Educators always assume that the biggest obstacle in the classroom is that the kids won't get the lesson or they'll do something wrong. What worries us the most is what the adults do wrong.

We've had Leader Study Groups on finding the main idea in fiction and non-fiction works, adding rigor to writing lessons, and stimulating kids' imagination and creativity with blocks. (Yes, wooden blocks. For more about blocks, see Chapter Five.)

Our 2010–2011 Leader Study Group topics included the following:

- Demystifying Rigor: Identifying Qualities of Excellent Teaching

- Quality Books and Adults Who Understand Them

- Don't Forget the Why: Lifting the Level of Teacher Practice by Preaching Purpose

- Excellent Reading Direct Instruction: Closing the Deal in Ten Minutes or Less

- Shared Text Day One: English Lit Seminars for Five-Year-Olds

- Upping the Rigor of Our Writing Mini-Lessons

- Leading with Efficacy: Leveraging the Teacher Improvement Cycle for Maximum Results

- Honing Our Powers of Observation: Seeing All the Right Things When Speed Observing

- Upping Our Game Around Book Discussions: Preparing and Executing Compelling Conversations

- Raising the Bar: Lifting the Level of Studying for the Adults

- Study Smart: Teaching Teachers to Study with Efficacy

- Volume and Quality Matter: Upping Urgency Around Independent Writing

- Short, Not Stupid: Treating Kids as Highly Intelligent

- Coaching for Greatest Impact: Running a Phenomenal Labsite

- Blocks: Building a World Without Achievement Gaps

- Fast: Observing

- Fast: Debriefing

- Fast and Direct: Teacher Feedback

The session on writing rigor was directed not at moving the scholars' writing up a few notches, but at helping the teachers markedly improve the quality of their model writing. Here's a closer look at what went on in the Leader Study Group on Upping the Rigor of Our Writing Mini-Lessons:

At 8:15 on a morning right before the Thanksgiving holiday, Arin, the Success Academy principals, and several of their deputies gathered in the office of Success Academy Harlem 4's principal, Danique Loving, to spend four and a half hours grappling with how to instruct and inspire their teachers to choose better topics and write more vivid and compelling stories when modeling good writing for their students' benefit.

The goal of this Leader Study Group was twofold:

- To prepare the principals to go back and lead implementation meetings around writing and rigor

- To hone principals' skills at coaching teachers in real time

They watched before-and-after videos of a teacher who received extensive coaching about how to set high expectations, pick up the pace, and add intellectual spark to her instruction. The teacher's performance in the second video was noticeably improved. "She's using sophisticated vocabulary in a natural way," said Michele Caracappa, the Success Academy Bronx 1 principal. "Her intellectual spark and her excitement and urgency picked up," observed Paola Zalkind, a leadership resident at Success Academy Harlem 2.

"The more spark, the more the pace picked up," said Arin.

"That comes from studying and knowing what you're saying," said Paola. "When you do know what you're saying, then you're not stopping as much."

"The more we can buoy their studying and confidence on the front end, the more that nets us rigor on the back end," said Arin.

The principals broke into groups to analyze other before-and-after videos, watched a lesson taught by one of Success Academy's best teachers, and then crafted advice to give teachers for an upcoming lesson on how to come up with ideas for small-moment stories. This kind of writing, for which kids choose a really pivotal and brief moment and then "zoom in" and write about it, is called a small-moment story. So instead of writing generally about the trip to the park, for example, a child writes about the moment he fell, after play sword fighting with a cousin, and ended up scraping his knee. The point is to get kids to unpack the micro actions and convey a central idea about them. At Success Academy we believe that to teach the children to write these stories, you first have to teach the grown-ups, and the grown-ups need to practice. "You just have to write honestly and choose something you're excited about," said Carrie Roby, then a leadership resident. Another commented that writing "is one of the hardest subjects to teach" because many adults and children alike find it so difficult.

Later they brought in a trio of third-grade teachers and worked with them on how to make their model writing more sophisticated. They concentrated on just two of the aspects of rigor: doing the thinking beforehand and figuring out how to add intellectual spark to the lesson. They did teachbacks with each teacher, practicing teaching the same lesson and getting feedback from the entire group, including fellow teachers. Some then went into actual classrooms and, under the principals' eyes, taught the small-moment story lesson to groups of children as a labsite. The verdict afterward from leaders and teachers alike was that all had moved their instruction up a notch. Instead of just talking about writing, they spent more time actually writing and thinking out loud in front of the students. They also picked up the pace. While the enthused teachers returned to their classrooms with next steps to work on, the leaders repaired to Danique's office for their own debriefing.

By drawing the teachers into the discussion, the leaders had gotten the rigor message across "without saying, 'What's rigor? What's rigor? What's rigor?'" said one leader. The teachers gained a better understanding of how much their model writing influenced the quality of student writing. They recognized "that if we want the kids to write in a more sophisticated way, then we need to first think how we are going to do that as grown-ups," another leader said. The leaders pointed to an insight that one teacher came up with on her own: "If you don't have good ideas, the rest could be a disaster." And they applauded the teachers' shift to less talk and more writing.

After a short break, the leaders dove back into the rigor seminar, this time concentrating on kindergarten and first-grade teachers. They began by watching a videotape of a teacher writing in front of her first graders at Success Academy Bronx 2. The teacher on the screen was having her students repeat instructions sentence by sentence. She somewhat laboriously talked about several personal stories she had shared with them earlier, then set out to retell the one about accidentally dyeing her hair green. "It makes you guys laugh. That's why I really like this one," she said.

It didn't make the leaders laugh. "Her teacher voice wasn't great," said one. A second said, "It was very choppy: 'Today we're going to choose a piece that's meaningful for me. Repeat after me . . .' A rigorous lesson flows like a conversation. She made everything sound like a procedure."

"That's not the level of sophistication we want to model for our scholars. It was 'I'm the teacher, you're the babies,'" said a third. "Clearly, we're the experts, but we want to draw the students into the discussion to be experts with us." Next the leaders brought in a group of kindergarten and first-grade teachers and critiqued more videos. Leadership resident Sean Cain at Success Academy Harlem 1 modeled how not to tell a good story about the time he ripped his pants on the way to work. He spoke in a monotone and began almost every sentence with "I." His pants ripped as he headed out the door of his apartment, and he simply turned around and changed into another pair. "Did you see how I got an idea for my story by thinking of something that was funny?" he asked.

"Funny for you, not for us," a teacher remarked.

"It wasn't genuine. You weren't sure of yourself. You hadn't mastered the lesson," said a principal. Sean readily agreed, saying, "Kids can understand when we talk fluently." Arin exhorted the teachers to tell the kinds of stories with which they would regale friends at a cocktail party. This prompted an outpouring of ideas from the teachers: "When I rode a camel in Pakistan." "When my homemade bread didn't rise at Christmas." "The sadness I felt when my older brother went off to college." The leaders had the teachers take a few minutes to write their small-moment stories in big letters across three pages, as they would expect students to do.

But even after the pep talk and Sean's example of what not to do, most of the stories, like that one teacher's bread, fell flat. The teacher who had vacationed in Pakistan wrote about her apprehension, but never actually described what it was like riding the camel. "Put in the feel of the camel's hair," advised Sean. Beth Davis-Dillard, another leadership resident at Success Academy Harlem 2, suggested striking a more conversational tone and telling the story like "it's really coming from your gut." The story about the bread fiasco on a trip back home to Kentucky for the holidays ended melodramatically, "When I saw what was in the pan, my heart sank. 'I guess there'll be no bread at Christmas.'" ("A Dickensian story," said Sean, who suggested having the bread flop by the end of the first page and allowing the story to unfold from there.)

The model writing clearly was still a work in progress. But Arin counseled the kindergarten and first-grade teachers, "Give yourselves license to take risks. Set the bar high—if everybody gets it, then the bar's not high enough. Have fun with your model writing, make it really rich and meaningful to you, and see what happens."

Again, there was a palpable sense of excitement among the teachers about getting this personal training from principals and leadership residents.

"A couple of us were saying that [before] we really felt locked into the lesson plan and couldn't miss a beat. Now we're trying to make it more authentic and make it our own," said one teacher.

"Just having the opportunity to have a dialogue about it was very helpful," said a second. And a third teacher said she planned to write about deeper and more sensitive topics than puppies or trips to the amusement park. "I sometimes stayed away from certain topics because I wasn't sure they would be completely appropriate, such as a death in the family," she said. "But even if it's a little shocking for them to hear from me for the first time, it might engage them more and encourage them to dig deeper into their own experiences and ideas."

"You might be surprised at the ideas kids can connect to. Their lives outside of here are really big," said Danique.

A couple of weeks later, as Paola Zalkind prepared to sit down with her school's first-grade teachers to hone their model writing, she reflected on what she had taken away from the Leader Study Group on rigor. "I told the teachers we were working with there that [the practice session] was much more important for me than it was for them. I hope we helped them," she said. "But more than anything, having that chance to get away from my building, sit with other leaders who do what I do every day, watch the videos, and identify the big issues makes me feel so much more confident to come back and do that by myself with my team."

Michele Caracappa said, "That's the key lever behind a lot of what you see at Success Academies. None of us feels that we're in this alone. It's not just about kids' learning. Part of what we are trying to build is this community of learners."

It's that ripple effect that makes the Leader Study Groups so worthwhile. They help the principals and other leaders step up their game, and they help both the teachers they work with that morning and the teachers back at their respective schools. The Leader Study Groups are an embodiment of our belief that the key to providing a world-class education is ensuring that the adults are learners too.

T SCHOOL

New teachers' first introduction to Success Academies now comes in an intense, four-week-long training session we affectionately call T School—the Teacher Success Academy—which began in July 2011. We also have our principals attend the parallel Principal Success Academy for eight weeks. In addition, teachers receive the equivalent of nine more weeks of training during the school year. This intense focus on adult learning, we believe, is the key both to our success and to dramatically improving public education.

Both the volume of training (the number of hours, days, and weeks) and the nature of this training are extraordinary and unprecedented. It all focuses on competencies and mastery and changing adult practices in order to change student outcomes. Almost every school, good, bad, or indifferent, offers teachers some training before school starts, although in many cases it may just consist of a few extra days, some of them spent decorating classrooms. We bring our new teachers together for a week off-site, usually at a college campus (yes, they sleep in the dorms), and then spend three more weeks teaching them the Success Academy techniques for high-quality teaching. The newcomers first spend hours working with our leaders, and then back at our schools they get to practice teaching with students attending our summer school and work closely with the leaders and returning teachers. We also pay our returning teachers to spend approximately four weeks before classes start in training and sharpening their craft.

The proof of T School's value, of course, is in the year ahead, but in summer 2012 we plan to open our Teacher Success Academy to other charters and districts, and we hope to train close to seven hundred educators. We're going to add a second session of summer school to give them a laboratory in which to put our ideas to work.

Earlier in T School's first summer—actually even before classes for the 2010–2011 school year ended—we launched the first Success Academy Teaching Fellows Program, bringing in twenty talented college graduates for an intensive, paid, six-week immersion both in our schools and methods and in the broader public policy debate about how to radically improve American schools. Most of the fellows stayed with us to begin their teaching career in Success Academies, but others headed off to work in schools elsewhere or sought other ways to make an impact on education policy. We'll be expanding the Teaching Fellows Program fourfold in 2012 and launching a Principal Fellows Program to train future principals.

Both T School and the Teaching Fellows Program reflect what we see as a mission for Success Academies that is even larger than giving a great education to up to twenty-five thousand children in New York City (our projected enrollment when we hit forty schools). We see ourselves as a model for other schools looking not only to obliterate the achievement gap but also to educate all children to world-class standards. We envision T School filling the role that colleges of education have failed to assume: one of preparing new teachers to perform at a high level on day one, armed with deep knowledge, an arsenal of professional skills, and the determination and know-how to help all children learn. Our intense, immersive, school-based teacher training program could eventually become a formal graduate school program, offering teachers a hands-on way to earn their master's degree even as they make that commitment to continuous improvement and learning.

Although the importance of learning by doing is now widely understood and appreciated when we're talking about children, the vast majority of aspiring teachers still spend their days "learning" in lecture halls far removed from the real classrooms into which they will soon be thrust. At best, these aspiring educators participate in occasional, lightly supervised classroom work. At Success Academies we believe traditional teacher preparation programs are completely inadequate in terms of providing future educators with the intensive practice, real-time coaching, immediate feedback, rigorous assessments, and other forms of school-based training that are critical to their success. To make up for these shortcomings, Success Academy has developed a battery of pedagogical strategies that combine repeated, intensive practice with real-time coaching and immediate feedback that allow the teacher to rapidly improve the lesson. This is part of how one becomes a professional in other respected fields, such as medicine. Teachers at Success Academies undergo rigorous training because our work, like all professional undertakings, is complex and vital. As Arin told new teachers during an extended T School session on finding the main idea in passages they read with the scholars, "We're not going to pass Go, we're not going to move until we grown-ups get the main idea under our belt and have practiced, practiced, practiced and attained a level of mastery. You wouldn't give a doctor a scalpel until he was ready. This is your scalpel, if you will. So we've got to get it right."

T School fills a gaping need in the education world. As the international consulting firm McKinsey & Company noted in a 2010 report: "The U.S. does not take a strategic or systematic approach to nurturing teacher talent . . . [W]e have failed to attract, develop, reward, or retain professional teaching talent on a consistent basis."[1] We have designed the Teacher Success Academy to be a new model of teacher and principal training. For teachers, T School offers a demanding, rigorous, and profoundly rewarding experience that eliminates the feelings of professional inadequacy that many first-time teachers, and some veterans, feel when in the classroom on the first day of school. For their students, T School is a life-changer. T School challenges traditional notions of teacher accountability, and focuses beyond accountability on teacher efficacy. One reason that punitive accountability systems have failed in many traditional school systems is that teachers simply have not been given the training to hit higher benchmarks and be effective. T School changes that, demonstrating that teachers, with the right training and support, truly can become excellent at their job.

Success Academy Bronx 1 principal Michele Caracappa said the thing that impressed her new teachers the most at T School "was just how much time and energy we put into studying children's literature. Many teachers reflected upon the fact that in the previous [professional development] sessions that they had attended before they started working for Success Academies, they simply had not had the opportunity to read, discuss, and debate the ideas within the books that they would soon be reading with their students."

They also were struck by the firm admonition they heard from Eva about the importance of "understanding the why" behind everything we teach. Eva told them, "You can't ask people to do something and take it seriously if they don't know why they're doing it. And they've got to communicate it to the kids. We're not the CIA. We're not trying to keep it secret from anyone what we're doing."

"We talk about the WHY, or the purpose behind the way we do things, constantly with our scholars," said Michele. "We tell them WHY a particular writing mini-lesson is going to help them make their story more engaging to their reader. We tell them WHY they need to speak 'loud and proud'—so that others can learn from their brilliant ideas!"

"At T School we get to focus on the why for the adults," she added. "We spend weeks ensuring that our teachers deeply understand the purpose of the way they will be teaching literacy, and also working to create a culture where it's unthinkable to teach a lesson without deeply understanding its purpose and thinking through how it will make our scholars that much more talented as readers, writers, and thinkers."

REACTIONS TO T SCHOOL

T School was an eye-opener for Alison Candamil, a new third-grade teacher at Success Academy Harlem 4. She previously taught in Brooklyn for three years. "T School was like no other experience I've ever had," she said. "I thought I had a credible handle on my craft. Reflecting back, I am realizing that this is just the beginning of my learning."

"In my previous experience I got little, if any, professional development," she continued. "The practice teaching with leaders and other teachers was especially valuable. It's flabbergasting to me how I ever functioned without these supports. If you're going to be successful at something, you need to practice it. It's not reinventing the wheel, but it's certainly putting a more efficient spin on it."

Hallie Brooks, a newly hired fourth-grade teacher at Success Academy Harlem 4, who previously taught English as a second language in Israel for two years, said, "I learned more in the month of T school before school officially started than I learned in four years of undergrad and two years of graduate school. This training experience far exceeded any other I had before. I truly believe that it made me the best teacher I can be, and with each session of T School that continues I feel myself growing as an educator."

Zoe Fonseca, a kindergarten and then second-grade teacher at Success Academy Bronx 1, said the professional development was "far superior to what most schools can provide." The entire network "is dedicated to increasing teacher effectiveness in a very real and time-sensitive way. What we learn one day, we are expected to implement the next," she said. She singled out the literacy sessions in which the teachers were pushed to analyze college-level texts with colleagues. "It wasn't always easy for us to reveal our own insecurities with discussing complex literature, but that type of passion for rigor is necessary if we are going to deliver the true message of college to our scholars," she said.

GETTING THE MAIN IDEA AT T SCHOOL

Unlike those in traditional teacher preparation programs far removed from the schools in which teachers eventually teach, our new teachers get to practice in Success Academy classrooms with students attending summer school and to work alongside our best, most experienced teachers, much like interns making the rounds with top doctors in a hospital.

T School places great emphasis on preparing the new teachers to teach our fast-paced and demanding THINK Literacy classes, with an emphasis on the following:

- *Mastering content*. We ingrain in teachers the habits and skills they must have to understand at the deepest level the books and other materials before they teach them to students. They learn how to analyze and ask penetrating questions about children's literature as if they were studying for a college seminar on English literature. Our teachers get ample time to study and plan on their own, but they also do so as a team, preparing lessons with colleagues at daily study and implementation meetings.

- *Witnessing highly effective instruction*. New teachers get to witness highly effective teaching by observing live classes and by watching videotaped classes from our EduTube digital library (a repository of more than fifteen thousand YouTube-like videos of internal "best practice" techniques). They also practice teaching under the eyes of master teachers and mentors and learn how to accept direct feedback.

T School training lasts about four weeks during the summer and the equivalent of nine weeks during the school year, with the exact length of time and type of training depending on the educator's level of experience and whether he or she has already taught as an associate teacher in a Success Academy. This training continues throughout the academic year, with each teacher receiving more than four hundred hours of professional education and instruction of the highest quality, which is the equivalent of more than a year of postgraduate coursework. Like everything else we do, T School moves at a fast pace, with direct instruction on a particular topic never lasting more than thirty minutes.

Sample Schedule: A Typical Day at T School for Principals

Putting the Cycle of Teacher Improvement into Action

Goals

1. Participants will identify the main idea (the deepest level of meaning) of a text.

2. Participants will sharpen their lens for speed observation.

3. Participants will hone their coaching skills.

Intro

Why is it critical for the adults (leaders and teachers) to be able to identify the main idea of a text with precision? Why is it critical to teach this to kids? What does excellent instruction around identifying the main idea look like?

Section One: Speed Observations

8:30–9:00 *Speed observations (Round One):* Success Academy trainers take participants through a cycle of rapid observations in which they watch five main idea lessons in quick succession. Participants are coached on their powers of observation in real time.

9:00–9:15 *Debrief:* Success Academy trainers force-rank (put in order of excellence) main idea lessons based on the qualities of excellent guided reading instruction.

9:15–9:45 *Speed observations (Round Two):* Participants cycle through another round of speed observations in quick succession.

9:45–10:15 *Ranking:* Participants force-rank lessons and defend their rankings.

10:15–10:45 *Video analysis test:* Participants study and analyze a series of main idea lessons using training films from our collection.

10:45–11:00 *Break*

Section Two: Studying the Main Idea

11:00–12:45 *Study meetings:* Participants learn how to lead effective study sessions on identifying the main idea.

- Trainers lead participants through a study session on identifying the main idea if they are teachers.
- Participants are tested in writing on their ability to identify the main idea.
- Participants receive direct instruction on how to lead an effective study session.
- Trainers lead participants through planning for an effective study session on identifying the main idea.
- Participants lead other participants through study sessions while receiving real-time coaching and feedback from trainers.
- Participants plan another study session based on feedback and coaching.
- Participants lead teachers through study sessions while receiving real-time coaching and feedback from trainers.

12:45–1:15 *Break*

Section Three: Teaching the Main Idea

1:15–1:30 *Modeling lesson:* Participants receive training on how to model an effective lesson on identifying the main idea during guided reading.

1:30–1:40 *Teachers practice (Round One):* Participants model a guided reading lesson, receiving real-time coaching and feedback.

1:40–1:45 *Break*

1:45–2:00 *Teachers practice (Round Two):* Participants model a second main idea lesson, receiving real-time coaching and feedback.

2:00–2:30 *Effective coaching (Labsite 1):* Success Academy trainers model effective coaching of teachers during main idea lessons, then coach participants as they practice coaching teachers.

2:30–3:00 *Effective coaching (Labsite 2):* Participants model a main idea lesson for teachers, then coach teachers as they practice teaching a main idea lesson while receiving real-time feedback and coaching from trainers.

3:00–3:30 *Test preparation:* Participants prepare for the practicum test.

3:30–4:45 *Practicum test (putting it all together):* Candidates are observed in action and evaluated on the following:

1. Leading an effective study meeting on identifying the main idea

2. Leading a labsite on identifying the main idea in which candidates must

   a. Model an excellent main idea session

   b. Simultaneously coach four to five teachers as they lead main idea lessons for small groups of students

   c. Give clear and direct feedback to the group of teachers (because giving *group* feedback is generally more efficient and more effective than giving feedback to individual teachers)

4:45–5:45 Participants who failed the video analysis test receive another round of training in making speed observations.

It was eye-opening for our new teachers at the start of T School 2011 to see how much hard work teachers put in toward getting the main idea from stories, poems, and other pieces of writing we teach to children. The main idea session was scheduled to last six hours. It actually ran for a day and a half as the newcomers discovered just how hard it was for them to do something we expect children to do in class almost every day.

"Today's going to be hard, and you're going to feel frustrated, and you're going to get stuff wrong," said Arin. "That's OK, because all we ask of you today is that you really engage in this work, take it seriously, take risks, and try. There's a tendency sometimes to shut down when things are hard. Don't do that. Keep practicing and it will set you and your kids up for a phenomenal year of understanding great books."

And it *was* hard work.

The leaders and teachers dissected *The Lemonade Wars, Magnus Maximus, a Marvelous Measurer,* an Aesop's fable, the poems "Cricket" and "Pebbles," and more. We use a four-point scale to grade written responses summarizing the main idea of a text, with 4 being the highest score and 1 being the lowest. They saw how hard it was to get a 3, much less a 4. "The two biggest pitfalls in book discussions," Michele Caracappa told second-grade teachers, "are that either the kids are just giving a plot summary and not interpreting the meaning, or it's all interpretation, all big picture, totally out of the context of that book."

At the end of the afternoon, the new teachers took a main idea test on two fables, a short story, and a biographical sketch. Leaders stayed into the evening grading them. The average score was a 2.5. We revamped the T School schedule to add three more hours on getting the main idea the next day.

Michael Gentile, a newly hired teacher and part of our Teaching Fellows Program who was an English major and debater at the University of Kentucky, said afterward, "I don't think anyone had any idea that we'd have to spend this much time on [getting the] main idea. While frustrating, ultimately it's encouraging. They want us to know it at such a high level that we'll be able to teach it and help our scholars talk like we talk. I can't imagine [teacher orientation] works like that at a lot of other places."

"It's fascinating," said Cinnamon Stapleton, a novice teacher at Success Academy Harlem 4 who majored in psychology at the University of Sussex in her native England; was a fund-raiser for the British equivalent of Teach for America; and then moved to New York, signed up for Teach for America, and was hired by Success Academy to teach third grade. "It's a huge learning curve for me, but I can see it's very effective."

Aristotle said it first: "We are what we repeatedly do. *Excellence,* then, is not an act, but a *habit*." T School is all about cultivating that habit.

TAKEAWAYS

Here's a summary of our advice for principals, teachers, parents, and school reformers who want to follow our path and focus relentlessly on the grown-ups to achieve excellence in their schools.

PRINCIPALS: You must build this schoolwide ethos of focusing on teaching and the adults. It needs to go without saying for everyone involved in delivering and overseeing instruction that the adults are the point of leverage. Practice what you preach by coaching the teachers, not fixing kids, when you enter classrooms.

TEACHERS: You've got a right to be professionally developed. Insist on it. Take advantage of every opportunity to improve your practice. If the principal and assistant principals aren't helping, ask them why not. Look to your colleagues for mentors and role models, and establish yourselves as a learning community. Recognize that setting a low bar destroys children's futures.

PARENTS: See for yourself what is going on in your school and in your child's classroom. (We have an open-door policy at Success Academies, so parents can visit at any time.) Is the teaching excellent? Is your principal focused on the quality of the teaching or consumed by other matters? Look for the investment in the adults and the quality of student learning.

SCHOOL REFORMERS: Focus on the adults and the barriers to their training and preparation. These include the inadequacy of schools of education and the massive regulatory apparatus forcing a race to the bottom in terms of teacher and principal quality. Teachers must have time to prepare, and they need rigorous, high-caliber training just like every other type of professional. Deprofessionalizing practices must end, or we cannot hope to give our kids the experience of being taught by adults who are knowledgeable and passionate about their craft.

CHAPTER FOUR

FAST

Putting Adults and Children on the Fast Track

Why are we in such a hurry? Why do we try to do everything fast in Success Academies? How fast are we? How does it affect teachers? What does it mean for the students?

Fast is a religion for us at Success Academy. It's a core belief, our gospel. It's an operating principle. It frames almost everything we do. Here's a partial list of the things we do at a pace that is unimaginable for most schools:

- **Fast** expectations
- **Fast** lessons
- **Fast** observations
- **Fast** feedback
- **Fast** diagnosis
- **Fast** solutions
- **Fast** implementation
- **Fast** improvements
- **Fast** sharing of best practices
- **Fast** adjustments in student reading levels

- **Fast** action on data and results

- **Fast** follow-up on school-based training

- **Fast** responses to queries, whether from parents, the network CEO, or other leaders

- **Fast** enrollment growth and opening of new schools

On the last point, our history testifies to how fast we've been growing. One school and 155 students in 2006 (opened eight months after Eva left the New York City Council and became CEO of Success Academy); nine schools and 3,600 students today; and, by summer 2012, fourteen schools and 5,000 students. On the horizon are forty schools and 25,000 students. Believe us, growing this fast isn't easy, although we're happy to say that each new school seems to be exceeding the magic of our first. But we feel that we've got to move this fast to meet the enormous educational need, whereby thousands must wait to get lucky and have their lottery number pulled. We also need to act fast because we want to point the way for other schools to turn things around.

Our belief in doing everything fast stems from the recognition that American kids, particularly kids from disadvantaged backgrounds, need to learn faster or we'll all pay a heavy price down the road. Already we're losing jobs to other countries that have dramatically upgraded the quality and capacity of their education system and, as a consequence, their competitive standing in the marketplace. Michele Caracappa, principal of Success Academy Bronx 1, explained it this way: "We want to make sure that kids are truly growing every day. If we really want our kids to catch up and compete with their more well-off peers, it needs to be productive time. We can't take it lightly. We need to make sure that we are really planning strategically for every minute." To make that happen, the grown-ups in school have to step up their game—fast. You can't expect the kids to move fast when the grown-ups are creeping along at a glacial pace.

Fast is not just more effective for teachers and kids, it's also more interesting. Adults forget how painful it can be for a child to sit through boring, plodding classes, doing the same work day after day at a snail's pace. Slow is boring and treats kids as intellectually impaired. A slow pace is often a sign that the teacher hasn't done his or her homework and doesn't really know the lesson. A briskly taught lesson shows the opposite: the teacher has done the thinking work in advance, knows his or her stuff, and quickly and engagingly moves through the material. We've got an obligation to make school interesting, and teaching at a quick tempo helps keep it that way.

It also has an immediate payoff, freeing up time for other interesting things. It's not just fast for the sake of fast. It's that we have other compelling goals we want to fulfill during our extended school day.

We believe that school is about so much more than academics and instruction. We want to make sure that we have time to build our classroom and school communities. We don't want to run short of time when it comes to establishing an ethical culture. We believe that schools are profoundly social places. We want our kids to have time to build friendships. Finally, we believe that kids should have time for all kinds of self-expression and that our schools should discover and nurture kids' special talents. It isn't just that we feel we're in a race to the top (although we do feel that way). We think fast is a lever that makes it easier for us to provide world-class schooling to kids who are working really hard and deserve nothing less.

At Success Academies we offer an enriched, highly progressive curriculum. If we're going to take the kids on all the field trips; if we're going to have time for science five days a week; if we want our kids to listen to classical music and learn how to play chess, practice karate, and experience other worthwhile things that will enhance their lives, then we have to teach the other core subjects fast or we'll run out of time. Yes, we have a longer school day and school year, but we do so much that there's still barely time to fit everything in. We also think recess—plain old playtime—is an important part of the picture. The classes, the outings, the community circles all play a part in making school such a magical place that the children cannot wait to arrive each day.

Go into our classrooms and watch a typical THINK Literacy lesson. The teacher spends only *ten minutes or less* delivering direct instruction on each lesson. We even call them mini-lessons. The rest of the time is given over to guided reading, read alouds, shared text, book discussions, and long, long stretches during which the scholars are reading and writing independently while the teacher coaches them in small groups. All the time spent on direct instruction in the course of seven hours of daily time in class adds up to seventy or eighty minutes at most.

That isn't a lot of time, of course, so every minute is precious. It's imperative not only that the teacher be highly engaging and well prepared to teach these fast-paced lessons but also that the scholars be listening and giving the teacher their full attention. If a child isn't actively listening, even the greatest instruction in the world goes for naught. We take great pains to give our teachers the know-how to make sure the entire class is listening actively during every lesson. In a class with 100 percent active listening and what we call edge-of-your-seat learning, the teacher can take the kids further, faster. Teachers conserve their energy and spend far less time reteaching. They tend to think they have to reteach a lesson because kids simply didn't or couldn't get it on the first bounce. Actually, much reteaching occurs because the teacher did not have the scholars' full attention the first time. Faster with full and active attention beats slower with a wayward focus, every time. And, as we said earlier, when looking for answers to nagging problems in the classroom, always look first to the grown-ups.

HOW LONG SHOULD IT TAKE?

Like educators everywhere, we start each year with a good idea of where we hope the students will be in nine months. We have a curriculum that sets out in blocks what they should learn and when. But we do something that isn't heard of in most other schools. We look at each unit and ask: How long does this *really* need to take?

In the guides that accompany math textbooks, it seems as if every topic is slated for three weeks. That defies sense. We know some things are harder to teach and learn than others. But who was the mastermind who made all these mystifying decisions about the proper length of time? Should we let that judgment trump ours when we're in a much better position to know students' capabilities?

The problem we're dealing with is that the pace is very slow in most schools. It is almost as if the publishers are producing curriculum materials for dysfunctional schools and expecting every other school to follow the same recipe. The expectations for what can be taught and how much children can learn almost always err on the side of slowing or dumbing things down and trying to skirt the hard thinking work. We deliberately go in the opposite direction, encouraging teachers to make it more rigorous but also more engaging and much, much quicker.

Outside of education, the real world marches to a much faster beat. The countries that are starting to outcompete us work fast. You can outsource a problem to a software shop in India in the evening and have an answer in your inbox the next morning.

But things slow down when you enter the K–12 world. We're not at all opposed to summer vacation, but schools spend gobs of time reteaching the stuff that children learned earlier then forgot. The pace of instruction is calibrated not to the kids at the top or even in the middle, but to the students at the tail end of the curve. The prevailing wisdom is that if the teacher goes faster, those kids will get left even further behind. We recognize that some of our scholars need more time to keep up. It's why we have an hour of free tutoring after school four afternoons a week, and why we require some students and their parents to spend an hour in Saturday Academy. We help them catch up without slowing down everybody else.

Charter schools have the freedom to move by their own clock. But even in the more innovative charter world the emphasis has been on simply more time and using every moment. The emphasis has not been on pure speed. But speed is a very important variable in learning. It is important for children because the lack of speed is the source of much of the sheer boredom you can find in most schools. Speed is important for the adults, too, because it is a key part of efficacy. If material can be mastered quickly, why take forever to do so? Success is about speed and mastery.

In the early days of Success Academy, while we were still shopping around for a more challenging reading program for kindergarten and beyond, Eva paid a visit to an excellent school and asked the principal how long it would take to implement balanced literacy at a high level. "His answer was five years," Eva recalled. "I said to myself, 'Five years! Oh, my God! My kindergartner is going to be ten, eleven years old. I don't have five years to wait. Five years to initiate something just doesn't work.'"

So we take pains to recalculate how long we think it should take to teach every part of our curriculum. If it has to take five years—if it's that good and that hard—we're not against that. But we really want to know for certain that it takes all of five years.

Now, the really hard stuff doesn't happen overnight. The standard for fast is not the same for everything. You can't become a phenomenal writing teacher tomorrow. The kids can't master finding the central idea of a story or poem in a week. One does not become a great teacher or a great principal in a year. It takes time and practice, practice, and more practice. Every new school we open has had to work methodically to get the basics right before it gets up to speed on the stuff that is really hard to teach. Writing falls into this category. It takes time. Sometimes you just have to keep chopping wood and have faith that you'll get to the end of the pile. Worthwhile goals take a long time to accomplish, and the values of steady, hard work and stick-to-itiveness are important to us. But fast as a philosophy and attitude helps get you there.

The culture of fast extends to everything we do. It's a customer service orientation, too. We expect our teachers to get back to parents promptly after they call. We communicate with parents in real time about their child's progress. We have this same fast service mentality when it comes to our teachers and the environment in which they work. When bulbs go out, we want them immediately replaced. When paint is chipping, we want our house of learning spruced up fast.

When a teacher's Smart Board malfunctions, we want it fixed fast. When teachers need more professional support, we expect school principals to get it for them fast. This attitude and approach goes all the way up and down the food chain. As we already mentioned, fast to us is a key part of efficacy.

EXHIBIT A: SPEED OBSERVATIONS

Exhibit A for our fast culture is the speed observations, the technique that principals and other leaders use to coach teachers and help them improve their delivery in the classroom. In most schools, observations are done a few times a year. A principal schedules a formal observation and will spend between forty-five minutes and an hour in a classroom. Then, a few weeks later, he or she will write that observation up and send it to the teacher or put it in the teacher's file. If it was a harsh write-up, the teacher may arbitrate the letter, which can take years. There is nothing speedy about the process.

We work at lightning speed. Teachers new to Success Academies quickly become accustomed to the sight of the principal and other leaders making their daily classroom rounds, staying five or ten minutes at most but coaching the teacher right then and there, out loud, with a whisper in the ear or even using a small earpiece. The principal doesn't just stay in the back entering observations in a notebook to discuss with the teacher later or to put in the file. He or she speaks to the teacher immediately, making timely interventions so the teacher can make rapid adjustments. It's like a football coach conferring with the quarterback on the sidelines or over a headset during the huddle, except our coach is there in the middle of the play.

Carrie Roby taught in the Bronx for four years before coming to teach our first class of second graders at Success Academy Harlem 1 in 2007. She became a leadership resident and now is principal of Success Academy Upper West. She remembers that it took a while to get used to all the scrutiny and instant feedback in the classroom. "At first my thought was, 'What's going on? Why are all these people here?' Doing the speed observations, they're in, they're out. What just happened? But it sort of stuck that that was the way we were going to do things." With the real-time coaching and feedback, there is no mistaking what you have to do to up your game ASAP. "It was much more transparent. It wasn't like you ever had to wonder, OK, am I on the right track? Is this what I'm supposed to be doing? You just would always know," Carrie said. "You felt, OK, I'm going to try to do all these new things."

The authors frequently join the principal and leadership residents on speed observations of THINK Literacy classes in every school and every classroom in the network—a feat only possible if the observations are quick and to the point. We arrange in advance for all the teachers of the same grade to be teaching the same reading lesson at an appointed hour, then blitz through as many as a dozen classes in roughly sixty minutes, huddling with the principal and others on the leadership team immediately outside each classroom to discuss what we had just seen, and then sitting down later to discuss the big picture, make a diagnosis, and come up with solutions to problems that may have cropped up in several classrooms. Then we agree on the next steps for the principal and teachers to take to quickly address the problems, which might range from low expectations to classroom management issues.

For instance, there was a morning in January, 2011 at Success Academy Harlem 2 when we joined the principal, Jim Manly, and his team to observe reading lessons. It was almost impossible for the visitors to hear the conversation about Roald Dahl's *Matilda* in Montclair, a second-grade classroom, not only because a radiator was hissing loudly but also because the scholars were mumbling or speaking so softly as to be inaudible. (Even before exiting the classroom, Eva fired off an e-mail on her BlackBerry to the building manager to get the radiator fixed.) The children had lots of opinions on whether it was right for the schoolgirl to use her telekinetic powers to exact revenge on the mean headmistress, Miss Trunchbull, but their comments were mostly lost to the world.

"It should not be the case in late January that the volume and the mumbling is what it is. The whole point of doing book discussions is for kids to be able to hear one another," Eva told the principal and a leadership resident outside Montclair. "To me it looked like 40, 50 percent of the kids couldn't hear. I couldn't hear. Our kids are going to be hindered by mumbling. We should have an all-out war on volume and mumbling."

Things weren't much louder in Ottawa, a third-grade class in which the discussion was about *The Raft,* a book by Jim Lamarche about a boy's change of heart on a summer spent at his grandmother's remote cottage in the Wisconsin woods. When the principal cupped his ear, the teacher urged her scholars to "be loud like at recess."

"Be loud and proud," said Arin. "Your whole life, when speaking in public or going on college interviews or a job interview, if you mumble that's going to hinder you. You have to put your ideas out into the world as if you're proud of them." The conversation immediately got louder.

A memo went out later that day asking all principals and leaders to turn up the volume networkwide. Fast.

The speed observations are a signature of Success Academies. They work on the same principle as speed dating or a recruiter's quick meetings with prospects at a job fair. The more you see, the better you are able to make the right judgment. Our observations last five or ten minutes, not forty-five minutes, but we do them over and over again. These rapid, repeat visits provide the principal and other leaders with powerful insights and paint a true and revealing picture of what is happening in each classroom. They don't have to wait until formal data reviews to see which classes and which teachers need to pick up the pace. We spot and fix problems on the fly before teaching habits are internalized. In addition, five times a year we give what we call Writing Prompt, whereby all the students in a grade do a short exercise that requires them to write for thirty to forty-five minutes. Then we bring a dozen or more teachers from all the schools together to grade the responses for consistency. Every principal and teacher in the network gets to see how every other school and teacher did by student and by classroom, and it gives us a fast way of knowing which teachers and schools need help the most.

HUSTLE IN THE CLASSROOM

We want the teachers to be fast in almost everything they do (except studying the books they teach beforehand—that takes time). Eva emerged from a slow-paced reading class one morning and expressed frustration that the teacher wasn't on her toes as she got her students ready for a half hour of reading in small groups. Eva remarked, "What the teacher should look like is a waitress hustling to each table: 'I love that the whole green table is thinking and reading; the yellow table is almost there. Almost everyone has their eyes on their book.'" Operating that way keeps the entire class on its toes and gives the teacher the vantage to see at a glance who is simply flipping through pages rather than actually reading.

Success Academy Harlem 2 teacher Amy Althoff was an embodiment of fast as she paced her second graders through a writing workshop bright and early one morning in her University of Chicago classroom. Their task was for each student to fill at least three pages with a story from his or her life. Ms. Althoff and associate teacher LeShonda Lopez buzzed about the room for the entire forty-five minutes, spurring the students on and proffering advice as they looked over shoulders. Ms. Althoff called out students' names and offered constant words of encouragement.

"I see David who doesn't give up. This is what we do every single day," she said. "Katerina has worn out her pencil. I can't wait to see the first person who asks for more paper . . . Ji is writing long and strong, never give up."

Ms. Lopez added her voice: "I see scholars reading their work to make sure it makes sense before they go on," she said.

"Look at that careful writing, those graceful curves," said Ms. Althoff, hovering above a boy's desk. "He's going to write a true story with a beginning, middle, and end. He's going to use everything he knows about writing great stories. Look at that . . . I see some third-grade writing. You are writing loud and strong. You keep writing and writing and writing." The two teachers kept a steady eye on the works in progress even as they danced around the room.

"I see some good ones," said Ms. Althoff. "You still have plenty of time to keep going and going and going. Look at Tyler. That boy does not give up. Look at Katerina. This girl is going to need another piece of paper, she is writing such an amazing story . . . Use everything you know about great stories. Keep going. Justin, your focus is amazing."

As the clock ticked down, Ms. Althoff stayed in constant motion. "Scholars, you have sixteen minutes left," she announced. "Keep going, keep going, keep going. I see someone about to get their first extra piece of paper." She got a competition going to see who could fill the most pages.

But she kept an eye out for those going slower, as well. "Tyler, don't get frustrated. Give me your best effort and that will be good enough for me," she said. "No shortcuts on the road to college." With only minutes left, the exhortations never ceased. "This is the only time we have today. Try your best to finish in the next three minutes. Tyler, you're going to college. You're getting ready now." Finally a timer beeped, and the students put down their pencils.

The prolific Katerina, who'd worn out her pencil and needed extra paper, had written a vivid narrative of her birth, from womb to delivery room: "I started growing and growing and growing . . . [At the hospital] she had to push and push and push and she pushed some more. Until I came out. I had blued [blood] all over me. It was all red and gooey . . . I was warm as a dog's fur . . . Mom wrapped a blanket around me and Mom sang me a song to go to sleep . . . The dr. gave mom and dad candy for doing a good push out."

Tekwan, a boy with a perpetual frown on his face, titled his story "No Christmas." "Today is the last day of November. I am not having a Christmas. My granmama is not putting a tree up. She is angry. She is not feeling well. She is sad . . . She is going to put a paper on the door that says we are not having a Christmas. I am mad, very, very, very mad."

But Tekwan found an upbeat note to end on: "I do not care. I will play in the snow. I am going to make a snowman."

Other scholars wrote about a rare family trip out of town; about getting to see a World Wrestling Entertainment match in person ("It was a mearacal," the happy boy wrote); about a mother's pancakes. Nearly every scholar had filled the three pages with writing and pictures to boot. And in a few minutes, Ms. Althoff and Ms. Lopez were hustling through the next class.

MOVING TEACHERS AND STUDENTS FAST

We love fables, but we beg to differ with the moral of Aesop's "The Tortoise and the Hare." Slow and steady may have won the tortoise that race, but we prefer fast and unflagging. It's the cure for lethargy and loss of interest. Yes, there's a risk that the kids who are experiencing difficulty may find it harder at first. But with great teaching, they can catch up and thrive with the quick pace. We tell the teachers to have faith that the scholars will get it, if not on day one then day two or day three. Think of how you felt on the first day of French class in high school when the French teacher may have rattled on without your understanding more than a single word or two. A few days and a few lessons later, you started picking up the gist, and by day ten it was no longer Greek—or French—to you.

There's no French in Success Academies (yet), but the teachers have standing orders to pitch every lesson to a high level, high enough that it challenges even the top scholars in the class. With difficult material that requires a lot of hard thinking and lots of practice to master, we encourage the teachers to attend quickly to their highflyers, who will need only a little nudge to understand the lesson. The students in the middle aren't much harder to move. And moving the top and middle students so quickly frees up more time for the teacher to work with the stragglers who need the most help. This is all part of our culture of fast.

So is the way our principals and leaders counsel, coach, and work with their teachers on the quality of instruction. Here, too, leaders start with their high-flying teachers because they are so easy to move. A few words spoken at the right moment—the feedback offered right then and there in the middle of the lesson—or a quick follow-up e-mail or conversation after school may be all it takes for them to improve their delivery or gain a firmer grasp of the point of a lesson. The teachers in the middle, too, may need only a relatively short intervention. And that frees the principal or leadership resident to spend more time coaching and guiding those teachers who need the most help.

We have other ways to help the latter. The principal may practice teaching the next lesson with the teachers, or have one of the best teachers teach a couple of lessons ahead of the grade team so his or her colleagues can sit in or watch it later on videotape. They may visit another Success Academy to watch one of the network's top teachers. Our experience is that the teachers welcome the help and intervention. Almost invariably they get the picture and, with the leaders' help, get practical ideas for what they must do differently in their classroom. It's quick, efficient, and effective. There's no embarrassment or hurt feelings; for one thing, because we share test scores and other data freely across the network, the teachers already know where their class stands in relation to every Success Academy class in that grade. In Success Academy Harlem 5's first year, the principal, Stacey Apatov, saw that one first-grade class had the lowest writing scores in the network, whereas another first-grade class had the highest. "I said, 'Maggie. Kelly. You're twenty feet from one another. Work together,'" Stacey said. She also switched their coteachers, took the first teacher to watch classes in another Success Academy, and went herself to shadow the principals of the two Bronx Success Academies as they coached their teachers on writing.

"It's great to have the highest and lowest work together," said Stacey. "My teachers know it can be done. It's not that our standards are too high. They see that classes in those schools are doing it, and they're like, 'OK, that's great. I'm going to do it, too.'"

At Success Academy we think it's a tragedy for teachers to languish in their practice. This country has underestimated how painful and discouraging it is for teachers to be left to fail or not be given the guidance and support to get significantly better quickly. Stagnation, being unable to accomplish one's job at a high level, is one of the greatest sources of low teacher morale. Of course, accepting poor or anything less than excellent teacher practice is also deeply unfair to students and their families. Principals have a moral obligation to improve teacher practice fast. They must help teachers improve their instruction so that scholars improve each day in real time. Principals must ask themselves a simple question: If it were my son or daughter, would I want their education to be in the hands of this teacher for the next nine months? If the answer is no, then they've got to do something to help that teacher dramatically improve instruction, fast.

SHARED TEXT ON THE FAST TRACK

A standard component of most balanced literacy classes is shared text, whereby the teacher and students read a poem or story together several times over in the course of a week, working out its meaning, identifying all its parts (stanzas, rhyme scheme, and so on), and putting the main idea into their own words. But whereas some programs may spend five days sharing a single poem or other piece of writing in this in-depth way, we do it in two to three days.

Leaders and teachers need to sit down and figure out up front how long something should take. If it turns out we were wrong, teachers spend more time on it. But we don't block out more than they think is necessary to get the job done in a fast-paced class. For a short poem, three blocks of fifteen to twenty minutes of reading time are usually ample. It's not that you get all the meaning you could ever possibly get out of it; obviously, the more time you spend, the deeper you can go. But we are very conscious of using the minimum amount of time to get the job done at a high level. Too many schools take the attitude that you've got all the time in the world. We don't.

Shared text is "like a mini English lit seminar" for the scholars, starting in kindergarten. On day one the teacher reads the poem to the kids, and then reads it with them fast. The teacher doesn't slow down, because we want to teach the kids to read fluently. Teachers have a tendency to slow down so the students can keep up. What we want teachers to do is set the fast pace and trust that the kids will keep up. They may not on the first and second days the teacher does it, but they will on the eleventh day. It's going to make them more fluent.

The structure for shared text in first grade is as follows:

DAY ONE: Understanding the Meaning of the Text

- The teacher reads the poem once by himself or herself, and then a second time with the students at a normal pace.

- The students identify the genre and how they will use it to determine the main idea.

- The teacher leads a discussion about the meaning of the passage, with students citing specific evidence from the text to support their ideas.

- Based on those ideas, the teacher writes a succinct, precise main idea in front of the scholars.

- The students then take their own crack at writing the main idea. The teacher quickly goes around the room and grades their efforts on a four-point scale.

- The students revise their main idea. If they got a 4 the first time, those students coach classmates who got a 2 or 1. The teacher scores them again.

- The teacher puts up a "bull's-eye" main idea and reviews it with the scholars.

DAY TWO: Focusing on How the Author Conveys Meaning

- The teacher and scholars quickly review the genre and main idea from the first day.

- The teacher reads the poem to—and then with—the scholars.

- They spend the rest of the twenty minutes discussing how the author uses ideas, structure, details, and mechanics to convey the main idea.

DAY THREE: Demonstrating Comprehension Through Writing

- The teacher repeats the steps from the second day (reviewing the genre and main idea, twice reading the poem).

- The teacher poses a question about the poem and gives the scholars ten minutes to write their response. Early in the year, in kindergarten and first grade, they may draw their response, too.

- The teacher reviews an excellent example of student work with the scholars.

The students quickly get accustomed to recognizing the genre of writing at a glance; reading each piece several times; breaking it down for meaning; understanding how the ideas, structure, details, and mechanics convey that meaning; and then capturing the point of the poem in their own words. Shared text isn't just about helping students become good, sharp readers; it's also about honing their critical thinking and writing skills. It's the key to their future writing success.

Spending five days reading and deconstructing a poem or text might yield richer insights, but it might not. The students may be muttering on day four, "Oh, no. Not this again." We're not working on Tennyson's "Ulysses" or Eliot's "The Love Song of J. Alfred Prufrock" here, much less Dante's *Divine Comedy*. We are dealing with excellent children's poems and passages from great books, and we're giving the scholars the tools they need to understand, break down, and appreciate other longer and more complex pieces of literature. Once they have learned to become great readers, they can teach themselves anything.

FAST IMPROVEMENT FOR HUMDRUM MODEL WRITING

Teaching children to write—not the mechanical process, but the thinking one—poses special challenges. Here our culture of fast bumps up against the reality that there is no shortcut to becoming a great writer. It takes practice to develop the skill of writing gracefully, cogently, and prolifically. Even voracious readers may find it difficult to take up their pencil or pen and put in writing the deepest meaning of a poem or passage they have just read. Yet we expect students to do this every day, and often several times a day, in class. In kindergarten and the early grades we constantly call on them to write about meaningful moments in their young lives. This is tough. It's tough for teachers, too, to consistently come up with great, interesting ideas for their own stories to model and write in front of the class.

On one round of kindergarten literacy speed observations, we hit a particularly dry patch. The lesson was about writing "expert" books, and one teacher after another seemed to struggle with making this interesting and exciting for the scholars. Their examples were dull: walking a dog ("Step One: Get a collar and leash"); going to Philadelphia (nothing about why one would want to get to Philadelphia—writing about how good the cheesesteaks in Philadelphia are, for example, would have been a lot more interesting); and scooping ice cream without making a mess (with an actual pint of Ben & Jerry's, but no samples).

It was clear that they needed more compelling topics. Eva asked the principal to have the kindergarten teachers reteach the lesson the next day, but this time to pitch it as if they were working with third graders. Because similar problems were cropping up in other schools, the same advice went out to kindergarten teachers across the entire network: try pitching the writing lesson as if your students were three years older.

The edict was greeted with more than a few rolled eyes. But a few weeks later, Eva got this note from a kindergarten teacher in the Bronx: "Many of us, including myself, were a bit skeptical. We worried that our scholars wouldn't be able to connect what we were showing them with the writing they needed to produce. We worried that rather than leaving them with something to build on, we would leave them confused."

But after adding sophisticated vocabulary, details, and a personal voice to her writing, this teacher noticed an immediate difference: "Scholars were engaged, and they certainly didn't seem confused. Over time other results have been apparent, as [they] begin to write with more complicated vocabulary, and greater volume; with humor and feeling; with a voice that is unique and speaks to what is important in each of their lives."

It was a fast turnabout with fast results. Now, we're not trying to teach quantum mechanics to five-year-olds (although they do learn some physics). But these teachers quickly saw that their students were capable of moving further and faster than they had previously realized. Slowing and dumbing things down is anathema to Success Academies.

THOROUGH AND EFFICIENT

New Jersey and a number of other states have language in their constitution guaranteeing every child's right to a "thorough and effective" education.

Nobody's constitution and certainly nobody's public school system promises or delivers an "efficient" education. But we're trying. Going fast is fundamental to the way we do it. The word *efficiency* simply isn't part of the lexicon for most educators. But we hear the clock ticking, and we have limited resources (charters in New York City get less money per pupil than traditional public schools). To ensure that kids meet our incredibly high expectations, we must teach every lesson at a phenomenally high level. That's why we do things at what looks like warp speed to educators long accustomed to working at a more leisurely pace.

We think all the time about how much progress we can make with our scholars in the next five days or two weeks or month. It's why when we spot something that's not working, we try to fix it that day.

The first and biggest payoff from doing things fast is that it is more engaging and interesting for both the teacher and the students. As we said earlier, it's an antidote to boredom and leaves the teacher more time to work with students one-on-one or in those small groups. Sometimes the teacher does go too fast. The solution then is simply to double back the next day and teach the same material again, perhaps with a different approach. We don't keep marching on and leave the kids behind. But our mind-set is that fast almost always beats slow.

Whatever the velocity of the instruction, sometimes a book discussion goes nowhere, despite the best-laid plans. We advise our teachers that when that happens, don't prolong the agony. Bring it to a fast end and start afresh tomorrow.

Time and speed really matter. We work hard at creating this culture in Success Academies, where everybody changes fast and in real time. It's hypocritical for the adults to expect the children to learn and grow exponentially unless they are willing to improve their practice just as fast. Further, principals cannot expect teachers to improve their practice on a dime if they as leaders are not fast in tackling problems and finding solutions. It's a given that our principals work super hard. But Eva also pushes them to be extremely aware of how efficient and smart they are about using their own time.

"It is not easy to know where your time goes or how to focus with laser-like intensity on the things that will most efficiently and speedily improve teacher practice," Eva emphasized in one memo. "It is easy not to delegate. It is easy not to follow a schedule and be constantly reactive. You need to determine how to spend your time and energy. Are you getting the biggest bang for your buck? Are you crossing things off your list fast and furiously so that you have think time? Are you managing your time exceptionally well?" She told them to reach out if they needed help.

We practice what we preach at Success Academies. We continuously review our schedule to ensure the most efficient use of time. Our teachers use timers and lead the scholars swiftly through setup routines. Success Academies were fast out of the gate when we started, and we're still accelerating. To get where we want our kids to go, our principals and teachers simply can't stop going fast.

TAKEAWAYS

PRINCIPALS: Don't buy the argument that teachers have to slow down to make sure all students "get it." Encourage your faculty to speed up and plan for the culture of fast. Show them how it's done. Give them time to see how the best teachers do it, and be fast in supporting your faculty.

TEACHERS: Pick up the pace of your instruction dramatically. You don't want to move so fast that large numbers of students are left behind, but realize that the bigger, everyday danger in most classrooms is that students will be bored out of their minds by a plodding, uncertain delivery. Recognize that if you're asking your students to learn fast, as a professional you need to up your game fast, too.

PARENTS: Keep a close eye on your child's school. Is fast a value there? Find out what and how fast your child is learning. Find out where your child is reading today, what the teacher's target is, and how fast the teacher hopes to get the students there. If it seems too easy and the progress is too slow, demand faster and better.

SCHOOL REFORMERS: GO FAST. Kids cannot wait. We need more fundamental reform, fast. But we also need to put policies in place that allow for schools to get things done much faster. If we're really going to close the achievement gap and give all kids an education that will allow them to compete against the eager learners in China, India, Singapore, and the rest of the world, we must insist that the educators also learn and grow fast. There's a race on for the future. Our schools must stop moving at a glacial pace. We need to make speed a core educational value and part of our public policy arsenal.

CHAPTER FIVE

RIGOR

Raising the Bar for Everybody

Rigor gets a bum rap.

The very word conjures up boot camp. We pride ourselves on the rigor of Success Academies, but the atmosphere and the ethos are the opposite of Camp Lejeune. Our schools and classrooms are joyous places, as bright and cheerful as Macy's at Christmastime. The kids love it; so do teachers and parents.

But here's the kick: they also love the rigor of what and how we teach. We challenge and push ourselves and our scholars to stretch themselves every day. We work longer and harder at it than is heard of in the public school world, and the kids are hungry for more.

Dionne Beckford, a teacher for eight years who then taught second grade at Success Academy Harlem 1 for three years before becoming a leadership resident, said, "I've never worked in a school like this before. The kids are thriving on what we're offering. They're just hungry for knowledge. They never complain about schoolwork. I could give them a pile of work to the ceiling and they'd dive right in it. If I give one child an extra work packet for enrichment or support, they're begging, 'Can I have one, too?' or 'Can I bring an extra one home?'" School, she added, "is fun, engaging. School is a place they want to be. They feel it's their second home."

If concentrating on the adults is our biggest contribution to the debate over how to make schools great, focusing on rigor is next. It is an innovation that costs little and pays big dividends. Simply by raising the bar and accelerating the expectations, you can make a revolutionary change in schooling. Because we're not barking out commands, you may not realize at first just how powerful this is. But stay any length of time, and its impact almost knocks you over.

We're obsessed with rigor in Success Academies.

What parents might find most striking is the energy, clarity, and enthusiasm of our teachers, and the high academic bar we set for kids while keeping that warm, loving feel that permeates our bright, cheerfully decorated classrooms. Learning happens at a fast pace, with substantial rigor, yet the kids are laughing and highly engaged.

Parents also notice the passion our kids have for learning, especially when it comes to reading. The classics of children's literature and wonderful new titles are everywhere. Kids read an enormous amount. As Jackie Albers, principal of Success Academy Harlem 1, told the *New York Times,* "We believe that if kids love reading, they can ultimately learn whatever they want to or need to."[1]

Prospective teachers, principals, and outside observers come into our class-rooms and marvel at what they see. There is a "What was that?" and a "How'd they do that?" reaction when a seven- or eight-year-old makes an eye-opening comment about *Matilda* or *The Lemonade Wars*. Beginning in kindergarten, scholars engage in a daily, dinner-table-style debate about a book, crafting argu-ments and marshaling evidence to prove their ideas. We believe strongly in letting kids do the heavy lifting of thinking rather than having teachers think for kids. Outsiders find the levels of thinking by even our youngest scholars both unusual and compelling. This looks different from almost everything else in education. It seems as if we are running a program for the gifted and talented or some sort of genius school, only because the intellectual demands, the thinking demands, we place on teachers and scholars alike so far outpace what is usually expected of kids in American schools.

Rigor is our answer to the vexing problems that plague public schooling.

So what's rigor? What makes a kindergarten class rigorous? First grade? Fourth grade?

Yes, it's THINK Literacy and the rest of the curriculum from math to science to the arts. But they are not the sole nor even the primary determinants of rigor in Success Academies. What really determines rigor is how high our principals and teachers believe the scholars are capable of going and where they set the bar every day in every class and every lesson. We're convinced that with great and inspiring teaching, our scholars can leap over extraordinarily high bars.

But this is difficult for adults, even for us, and even when it is part of one's core set of beliefs. We have to keep fighting the temptation to lower the bar so everybody can sail over it. It's almost human nature to want to avoid struggle.

Adults and children alike have that instinct. We have to wage a constant battle to embrace struggle.

That's not what most educators or professionals in other walks of life do. Our whole orientation is to find ways to do everything with more ease. So much so that struggle has gotten a bad reputation in education. Instead, we want every kid to know the right answer. We want simple formulas to remember. We want to teach strategies. But if one of the fundamental purposes of school is to teach kids to think, then this approach really does not work. We need to teach kids to ask great questions instead of simply to get the right answer. We need to teach children to work through a struggle and come out the other end with ideas, knowledge, know-how, and intellectual perseverance.

Teachers are taught in colleges of education and graduate schools that if every child quickly gets the answer, they are doing their job. But if every child gets it right away, why bother to teach it? It was too easy.

Rigor is a mind-set and an attitude about kids and their capacity to think and solve problems. It's a belief system. It's the conviction that we're harming kids if we don't treat them as smart and thoughtful. Everyone agrees that it's easier for very young children to learn a new language. Well, we think they can learn everything more deeply and faster than our country seems to give them credit for.

People commonly think rigor is simply about the curriculum. That's important, but what matters even more are the adults and the power of their instruction—and how effectively the teacher works to make the students think.

Rigor is a core value of ours. We think it is important. We believe in it for its own sake. We think it improves our community and the world around us.

It can be painful for any educator to hear he or she is not rigorous enough, especially in a well-organized, well-behaved classroom in which all or nearly all the students "get" the lessons and do the required work. But it has to be said, even if it is difficult for our schools to swallow. We are underestimating children daily, and we must stop it for the sake of our society.

To borrow a metaphor from Stephen Covey (author of *The Seven Habits of Highly Effective People*), rigor is one of our big rocks.[2]

In too many schools, teachers are, in a word, boring. It starts in kindergarten when the teacher adopts a singsong voice whenever speaking to the whole class. It's an insult to the scholars' intelligence. What the teacher is saying should be so interesting that the kids are sitting on the edge of their seat, hanging on every word. It's intellectual spark that holds and keeps their attention, not baby talk or, even worse, a monotone.

Clip 6 **Singsong Versus Spark**

The first segment of this clip shows a teacher infantilizing her second graders by using a singsong teacher voice and having scholars parrot back phrases. As evident by looking at the scholars' faces, the singsong teacher voice is kryptonite to rigorous, authentic learning. What's more, it is absolutely exhausting for anyone to maintain for nine hours a day! In the second segment, the same teacher is clearly just herself, no acting necessary, as she shares with scholars her passion for great writing. Put simply, she **talks to kids like they are smart,** and as a result they are totally hooked on discovering what great writing looks, feels, and sounds like.

Educators sometimes are oblivious to how boring school can be. A boring lesson and a boring book are torture for children. Teachers have to make this stuff interesting. They don't have to chew the scenery. Not all of us are stage personalities. But schools have underestimated their moral obligation to be interesting, compelling places. Principals and teachers must work at this, or the boredom will quickly creep back in. Making school interesting doesn't happen automatically, no matter how good the teacher. It takes a lot of work to be engaging, but it's also a lot easier with children in elementary school than with tweens and teens.

Jim Manly, principal of Success Academy Harlem 2, offered a definition of rigor in one of the "Weekly Update" newsletters he sends out to teachers and staff. He acknowledged that rigor can be a bit like Justice Potter Stewart's famous dictum about pornography: it's hard to define, but you know it when you see it. Jim went on to say that it was also a "moving target" because different children in the same class might very well be at different stages of development. He added, "The challenge of your work, then, is to consistently ask yourself the question, Is what I did today with scholar X or scholar Y more challenging, more sophisticated, more in-depth than what I did the day before?"

SCHOOLED NOT TO BE RIGOROUS

Why is it so hard for even the most talented teachers to be truly rigorous?

Chances are they've been schooled not to make instruction too difficult lest they discourage children and their frail, tender egos. Many of our teachers taught previously in schools with low expectations and dismal results. They may have been the exceptions to the rule at their old school, and they naturally assume they brought high expectations with them to Success Academies.

The problem is they don't actually know where the bar should be. In college and graduate school they were steeped in educational literature that spends so much time warning against doing anything that might not be "developmentally appropriate" that it seems almost a crime to aim above kids' heads. Our vantage point, however, is different. We think it's a shame and maybe even a crime to bore kids to tears and to underestimate their ability to think and reason. In our experience, kids are unbelievably clever and profound when given the opportunity to be so.

Many young teachers do not have children of their own, and perhaps that is why they are so uncertain about where the bar should be. In the absence of personal knowledge, they defer to those whom they perceive to be the experts. Also, there is such a consensus about what is "age appropriate" that it is hard to find people to argue with, and therefore teachers' views often do not evolve.

Unfortunately—tragically—the bar in most American schools is set perilously low. There is a race to the lowest common denominator such that the children in the class who struggle most establish the level of rigor. It's a sad truth that many kids who graduate from our high schools need remedial math and reading before they can start taking regular college classes. But this happens in elementary and middle schools as well. All too often this need for remediation determines where the bar is set. Publishers are selling textbooks to dysfunctional districts and literally are assuming (perhaps often correctly) that the kids in first grade have to repeat most of kindergarten math because they did not learn it the first time. Publishers imagine it takes a gigantic amount of time to teach something like fractions. The rigor bar suffers from prevailing ideas about not only what kids should learn but also how long it will take them to do so. It is as if no empirical evidence about how fast children can learn actually dictates the content or pace of learning.

Through no fault of their own, teachers, in schools of education and via curricular materials—the textbooks and resource materials created to teach reading, writing, and mathematics—have almost been conditioned to treat remedial instruction as the normal state of affairs in public education. Prior teaching experience in dysfunctional schools has reinforced that message. Finally, teachers are taught that they are successful when everyone gets it. If you keep the bar low, everyone will get it, ergo . . . you've got the American public school system.

Most teachers in traditional public schools are not familiar with what the children in the best schools, public or private—or what students in India and

China—are learning. They don't see what might be possible. Consumed by the here and now and the daunting task of merely surviving in schools awash in mediocrity or failure, they aren't spending much time asking themselves: Is what I'm teaching rigorous enough? Is this the best we can hope for? Our answer is a resounding no!

We must stand up for rigor because our children and schools are suffering. Our expectations are not just a little low, but rather profoundly off the mark. We are putting our children at a severe, lifelong disadvantage by failing to have high expectations for what they can accomplish intellectually, starting in kindergarten.

At Success Academy we are testing the ceiling, the upper limit of what children can learn and how fast they can learn it. We are searching for the highest level of rigor. This is not a theoretical question but an empirical one. We know that calculus for kindergartners is way too hard, but do we know how far exactly we can push kids' thinking on fractions in kindergarten? We would argue that we do not know the ceiling for students in each grade and that schools have a moral obligation to figure that out and not keep stultifying the kids.

The way the educational establishment works is to assume the kids know nothing until the grown-ups teach it to them. Not at Success Academies. We do a lot of pretesting to figure out who knows stuff before we start. We also see ourselves engaged in adaptive learning, meaning we use tests that allow kids to go on or stop when they have reached a ceiling. We like to avoid prejudging kids. We want to know how far kids can go intellectually. Then we spare no effort in moving them rapidly forward from where they really are starting.

We also see rigor and testing the ceiling as conducive to true educational justice and opportunity. This upping of the intellectual ante is the only way to close the achievement gap and banish the mentality that allows that gap to persist. Because our schools are colocated in the same buildings with traditional public schools, and because they draw children from the same neighborhoods, the difference is crystal clear to the parents and everybody else: our scholars are learning more, way more. They are on the road to college.

We want our kids to love school and find it a tremendously engaging, always interesting place, one where they can make friends and experience the love of learning and the excitement of being part of a thriving educational community. We also want them to achieve high levels of mastery not only in core subjects like reading, writing, math and science, but also in chess, art, music, dance, sports, and karate. You can't get there without rigor, and it is the adults' job to make sure that it is there.

We want everyone in the school to be as excited and enthusiastic about rigor as he or she is about our Halloween parade and party. Our teachers have sky-high expectations for how kids behave in class. We need them to expect just as much from the kids' intellects.

We focus on the adults, not the children, because the grown-ups have the power to create a warm, nurturing, orderly, academically rigorous environment—or not.

We're not shooting for perfection. That's unattainable. It's also often an excuse. This is a common misconception among educators who mistake rigor and exacting standards for perfection. At Success Academies we shun perfectionism and the perfectionist mind-set. Perfection is destructive. Perversely, it actually encourages playing it totally safe, not shooting for the stars. We're a place that takes risks and tries daring, new things. We're after continuous improvement, not the impossible.

We weathered a small storm in the middle of our 2010–2011 school year when we gave all the third graders an interim assessment in math over two days that was admittedly tough. One teacher—indeed, one of the network's very best teachers—sent Eva an e-mail voicing frustrations over the test. "I know we DO NOT expect every child to be able to correctly answer every question. I understand that we are trying to see if kids can take what they know and apply it to different types of problems and more challenging problems," the teacher wrote. "I agree that our curriculum needs to be more rigorous, but, even if we had made our curriculum more rigorous, some of the questions would be rigorous for fourth or fifth grade." She cited examples of word problems that demanded a higher level of skill than was customarily expected by the middle of third grade.

A couple of days later she got, not untypically, a 2,400-word response from Eva. "Although you are one of a few who spoke up directly to me about it, my sense is that many, many of your colleagues are uneasy about the topic," Eva wrote. Then she laid out the argument for rigor, rigor, and more rigor.

I view this topic as profoundly important: What mathematical concepts and facts and what kinds of problem solving mastery should we expect of our scholars, at what age, and how fast? Indeed this conversation goes to the heart of what we do. The conversation is about not only the content that we teach but also the standards we have for ourselves and the kids.

In our effort to build a better educational mousetrap, to have the best school design, a place that works exceptionally well for teaching and learning as well as for our parents, we are having to experiment and continually test out new ideas and new assessments. And that means try things, revise, and try again. It also means we have to fail and make mistakes. We are pioneering also because schools have not found what kids are capable of mathematically. Rather, a ridiculous number of assumptions have been made. Kids in Japan and Germany and Singapore are being asked to do much more rigorous math and at much earlier ages. The expected pace of learning completely outstrips what American educators are expecting.

Here in Harlem and the South Bronx we are doing what India did a decade ago. We are experimenting. We are trying to find the rigor bar. We are trying to develop a shared culture around struggle and challenge, both for the grown-ups and for the kids. Struggle usually means you are on to something critical, important. So although I do not mean this to come out the wrong way, I view teacher frustration with the math interim assessments as a good thing. It means we are on to something. It means that we are not in comfort zones.

The teacher's anxiety raised important questions:

- Are the assessments fair to kids? To teachers? To parents?

- Is it wrong for kids to be frustrated? Is it right for us to change a test to avoid kids' frustration?

- Should we be truthful to parents or avoid having them feel bad about their kids' performance?

- How do we encourage rigor and not make teachers feel scared and bad about the results?

- How do we build a culture of teacher curiosity so that everyone is eager to know what kids can and cannot do? How do we help teachers be adventuresome when it comes to kids' intellectual ceiling (as opposed to being focused on their floor)?

The wording of questions can always be improved, but it's still useful to figure out why the child got the wrong answers, and in real life kids will confront poorly worded questions.

We can all say we believe in rigor, but we need to identify standards and then test them out and see if we hit the mark. Let's suppose that the third-grade test was extremely rigorous, and that 50 percent of our kids did reasonably well and 50 percent bombed. That would be very useful. For the 50 percent who did well, that is an incredible discovery. Our previous work with them has been profoundly too easy. For the 50 percent who bombed, we shouldn't assume they did so because they could not get it or because they did not understand mathematics. It may be a focus or a reading issue, or one of poorly worded questions. We have to move away from the idea that tests and assessments are about fairness. That should not be our primary goal. Our goal should be an assessment that tells us what kids understand and are able to do—one that drives the grown-ups' ability to readjust teaching to achieve mastery.

We certainly do not want to have whole-school meltdowns, and we want to be sensitive. But we also need to toughen up. Yes, even little kids need to get comfortable with struggle and with not knowing the answer and working through it. We also need to teach kids to hold it together when they get overwhelmed. These are very important life skills.

Parents may get upset, but part of the problem is, frankly, that those in charge of public education were dishonest in years past. The parents were gulled into thinking their kids were doing exceedingly well, but the reality was that the standards were way too lax and the grading was too easy. This is exactly what happened with the New York State test. It is not fair to do this to parents. At Success Academies parents expect to be told the truth about their child's performance—and they are.

Literary Analysis in First Grade

Let's take a look at the discussion in a first-grade classroom at Bronx Success Academy 2 one morning, where teacher Sasha Growick and the scholars had just read *The Araboolies of Liberty Street,* an exuberant picture book and modern allegory by Sam Swope about the dull, strictly regimented life on a block dominated by two petty tyrants, General Pinch and his wife. Neighborhood life is turned topsy-turvy by the arrival in a rainbow-colored van of the noisy, madcap Araboolie family, who break all the rules and convince the neighbors to add color and fun to their houses and lives as well. When the general carries out his threat to call in the army to destroy the one house on Liberty Street different from the rest, it's his own home—now the only one on the block not painted in pastels—that gets destroyed.

Perched around the perimeter of their blue reading rug in Ms. Growick's classroom, the six- and seven-year-olds carried the conversation by themselves.

"How did the Araboolies save Liberty Street?" asked Amarosi, leading the discussion.

Allen answered, "If the Araboolies did not come, then they won't have any freedom, they'll just stay there in their houses doing nothing."

Amarosi then asked, "What do you mean by 'they need freedom'?"

Allen replied, "I mean they need freedom all the time, they're just stuck in their houses because the Pinches, they are in charge of everybody, but they are not in charge of everybody. Everybody has a different life so they could do whatever they want. The Pinches can't just control them."

The discussion coursed back and forth, with the children calling on one another and the teacher only occasionally chiming in with questions of her own. Vanessa Bangser, the principal of Success Academy Bronx 2, said there were discussions on this level every day in Ms. Growick's class in a school filled with students whose families are poor or do not speak English or both. The boy leading the discussion was classified as an English Language Learner; another qualified for special education. Despite a learning disability, that child "has brilliant ideas. The conversation wouldn't be the same without him," said Ms. Growick.

The conversation also would not have been the same if the children had not learned from their teacher how to marshal evidence from the book; hear each other out; and, when needed, challenge a classmate who isn't answering a question. The boy who contributed the most insights was a good reader when he started first grade, but it still took inspired teaching to get an entire class carrying on such a precocious discussion. Ms. Bangser had worked closely with Ms. Growick to push the boundaries of what both thought possible in first grade. The principal had challenged Ms. Growick to hold her peace and let the kids do the hard-thinking work. "It was a huge development for her to move to this point where you didn't see her in the conversation. That is not what her nature is. Her nature is to dominate the conversation," said Ms. Bangser. Ms. Growick "took that idea, struggled with it, and then ran with it. By the end of the year it caused her colleagues to reevaluate what they thought was possible. My teachers have exceedingly high expectations, but they were shocked by the level of the conversations kids were capable of having. It was an incredible feeling seeing your kids scale such heights."

 Clip 7   **Book Discussion, First Grade**

When watching this video it's easy to focus on what the kids in Ms. Growick's first-grade class at Success Academy Bronx 2 are doing. They are certainly impressive! Let's focus instead on what Ms. Growick has done to be able to remove herself completely from the book discussion, leaving her first graders to run it at such a high level. **First and foremost, Ms. Growick demands that the kids listen actively *to each other* 100 percent of the time.** Often schools make the mistake of having the standard be that kids *look like they're listening*. But kids can look like they're listening and not be learning a thing. In this video it's obvious that Ms. Growick has set the active listening bar much higher. Scholars lean in intently as their classmates speak, ask clarifying questions ("What do you mean by 'they need freedom'?"), and check that they are understanding their classmates' ideas ("What I hear you saying is . . ."). When you watch this video again, look for other specific evidence that kids are *really* listening to one another.

Choosing Rigorous Books

Books are a big part of the magic at Success Academies. Every classroom is swimming with great books. We are frequent shoppers at the Bank Street Bookstore, a jewel of a children's bookstore on Broadway near Columbia University that is operated by the Bank Street College of Education. Every time we visit the bookstore, Sarah Yu, who works there and is a walking encyclopedia on children's literature, wheels in a trolley packed with a hundred or more books of fiction, nonfiction, poems, adventures, sci-fi, and other genres for us to select from. Some are classics, some are classics to be, and all are good, engaging reads for children from five to eleven. With Sarah as our guide, we winnow the stack down to perhaps thirty and order dozens of copies for our classrooms. We could pay less by ordering them online, but that would deprive us of Sarah's expertise and that of her well-read colleagues. Rigor has a price, and it's worth it. Many New Yorkers regard Bank Street Bookstore as one of the city's treasures, but no other school comes close to "the extent of our relationship with Harlem Success," says Sarah.

RIGOROUS BLOCK PLAY

Perhaps nothing captures better our obsession with rigor than how hard we work at making playing with blocks an intellectual experience for our kindergartners, teachers, and school leaders. We hired Jean Schreiber, an early childhood education consultant, to come to our schools and teach our teachers about imaginative block play. We squeezed out scarce space in our school buildings so that each had a separate, dedicated lab room for kindergartners to play with blocks. We devoted an entire Leader Study Group to the topic of how to coach teachers to make block play as intellectually enriching as it is plain old fun.

Jean explained how high-quality block play can let creativity and cognitive development soar. Children learn about shapes and sizes and, as their first towers come tumbling down, something about balance, mass, and gravity as well. They learn to choose the right size blocks for their towers, bridges, and roadways, and gain motor skills, eye-hand coordination, and the ability to plan. They also learn to work with each other in tight quarters.

"Blocks are scary for teachers because kids can whack the other kid over the head with them. They make a lot of noise when they fall down," Eva said. "We're going to have to be braced and adventuresome, and we're going to have to train and support the kindergarten teachers. Leaders can't do that unless you are extremely confident and knowledgeable yourself."

After a short preliminary discussion, we trooped into the block lab at Success Academy Bronx 1 and watched Jean give a short lesson and guide the play of several children. Later on the principals got to play the role of teacher and coach.

"The goal of the mini-lesson is to show them ways to get a great idea to make their building. Most times children will just start to build without a plan when they go into the block area unless you've done a mini-lesson," said Jean. "I'm going to take it from the perspective of what an architect does, how they come up with their ideas by understanding how the building is going to be used, who's going to be in the building, etc., and then have them pretend to be architects with me. I'll have them quickly do drawings. I don't expect the buildings to necessarily represent what they put down on paper, but I want them to start thinking as they are building."

Jean gave the principals marching orders. "Don't jump in too soon. Let the child struggle a bit. Avoid asking, 'What did you build?' and instead ask open-ended questions, such as 'What can you tell me about the building?' or 'How does it work?'"

"A lot of times they really haven't built something they can name, and then they get very uncomfortable. Kids want to please adults," said Jean. "I almost never go in and give them the answer. I give them some tools and strategies: 'I wonder what would happen if you did this instead of this?'"

In the kindergarten lab, Jean told the children about her son, who is an architect, and invited the children to help her design and build a school.

"Think hard about what that building is going to be used for and what happens in your school. What are some things you need in your school building?" she asked.

"A big line so it can be straight," said Taniah.

"Straight walls," Jean interpreted.

"You need a big triangle for the roof," said Kamel.

"A triangle for the roof," concurred Jean. "What else?"

"You need a door so people can come in," Moriah said.

"What else?"

"You need windows," Taniah added.

In short order the kids decided the building would need a lunch room, a play room, classrooms, and a room for the teachers as well as hallways.

Jean stopped there and had the children think about and sketch a different building than they had in mind, choose their blocks, and set to work.

Fernando's "spider" tower (as he called it) rose and fell the fastest. "What are you going to do next?" Jean asked.

"Put it closer together," said Fernando as he laid four blocks for a bigger base.

The principals observing the block play session later saw two girls silently working on a castle from opposite ends and at cross-purposes. With a few words from Jean, they began talking and working together, moving from parallel play to cooperative play. After five collapses, Fernando got his reconfigured tower to stand up.

When it came the principals' turn to coach, they peppered the five-year-olds with questions, frequently interrupting their building. Jean counseled them afterward to go easy on the interrogations. "You don't need to be constantly talking and badgering kids with questions. When you see something that's interesting, challenging, frustrating, those are the times to go in," she said. "It isn't really necessary to find out exactly what the child is doing and why they are doing it. The end of block time while the buildings are still up is a good time to ask 'What was challenging?' 'How did you solve this structural problem?,' 'Why did you do this?' rather than being on their case while they are building."

In a fifty-minute period—that's how long kindergartners get in the block lab—there's always time to ask questions and help build children's vocabularies, Jean noted.

"We want to talk less but more strategically," said Arin.

Eva said she'd expected Fernando to get his tower built on the third try, not the sixth. But she repeated Jean's advice: "We need to teach our teachers to hold back. The kids will figure it out. Some will do it in three tries, some kids may do it in fifteen. But it's not like they're incapable of figuring out the length of the piece that goes across the top."

"You have to know how much risk they're willing to take," said Jean. "When they meet challenges, some will make those six tries, others will give up. If you'd been by their side, you can help them get to that stage at which they solve the problem."

Jean said children eventually can make signs for their temporary structures and construct stories about them "so it becomes a narrative that they can write down. Then you have that literacy piece that goes with the building."

Eva stressed the importance of generating conversations and getting the young scholars to talk more about what they are doing and learning, not only in block play but in every class. "If we don't have our kids talking more, we are not going to get to our end goal of college graduation. We've got to crack that nut, and it's going to be hard."

Two and a half hours had elapsed, and the principals were now fired up about block play and ready to take the gospel of rigor with blocks back to their respective schools and to expertly coach their teachers. Our principals regularly write memos and newsletters to their teachers sharing insights from the Leader Study Groups. That evening Michele Caracappa, the principal of Success Academy Bronx 1, took out her BlackBerry and shortly before 10 p.m. sent her faculty a missive headlined, "Why Blocks? Lessons for Us All!!!" It read in part:

As you may have noticed, there were an awful lot of people over the age of five years old in the lab room today. Jean Schreiber was here along with the principals of our seven Success Academies, and for two and a half hours we had the opportunity to focus all of our collective energy on nothing but blocks, blocks, blocks.

Why blocks? Through open-ended play, kids have the opportunity to develop in many ways. They begin to learn the principles of balance and stability as they create their structures. They experiment with symmetry and explore area and volume. They talk with one another as they plan their structures and work together, collaborating and negotiating to determine what should go where. They invent story lines about their structures, using their imagination to turn unadorned pieces of wood into whole new worlds.

Through block play, our scholars develop their critical thinking skills. They build oral language and vocabulary as they discuss their work. They get a chance to be creative—to explore new ideas, to experiment, to invent. This work (or play!) is a whole lot of fun, but it's also critical to our mission of closing the achievement gap and preparing our scholars for the world of college and beyond.

She told them about Fernando's tower, and concluded: "Struggle is a good thing. Blocks fall down . . . In working through it on his own, think of all that

Fernando learned. So often, as educators, we put on our Superman cape and rush in to save the day—to save scholars from struggle or frustration, or to fix their work in an attempt to remedy whatever was going wrong. It's important to remember how much kids learn through struggle! Sometimes the best move we can make is to just pull back and watch and see if our students can think through how to solve a problem on their own!"

Other principals wrote communiqués of their own, and soon everybody in the network was on the blocks bandwagon. Danique Loving, principal of Success Academy Harlem 4, said, "That's the beauty of having so many people to bounce ideas off. When you're left alone on an island, it's easy to get lost. If I was by myself, I might have said, 'Blocks are just for playing time.' But having that conversation with everyone made it clear that we need to make blocks as rigorous a time as possible."

LEADERS RAISING THE BAR

Rigor starts with leaders. Our principals and other leaders are the engine powering the rigor train.

Michele Caracappa, a founding first-grade teacher at Success Academy Harlem 1 before becoming principal at Success Academy Bronx 1, said, "We had an amazing team of smart and hardworking teachers, but . . . we had no clue how we could truly push kids to the level that we do now." Michele remembers proudly showing off end-of-year writing samples from her best first-grade students, who used dialogue and different voices in their stories. "There were certainly great elements in those pieces," she said. But now, with THINK Literacy's greater emphasis on writing, the young scholars across the board in Success Academies are writing far more sophisticated stories. "Looking at what our teachers are getting our kids to do now, it's almost embarrassing to think how proud I was of these [early] pieces. It's a testament to the work that we've done together because I think none of us alone knew what was possible," said Michele. "From day one in kindergarten we have kids writing across three pages. Setting the expectation level that high has dramatically impacted what our kids have been able to achieve."

Our two new Bronx Success Academies have large numbers of students from homes in which the parents speak a language other than English, especially Spanish. It was especially gratifying for us to watch the dramatic progress that both Michele Caracappa's and Vanessa Bangser's schools made in reading and writing with the rigorous THINK Literacy curriculum. Michele recalled that her newly hired, handpicked faculty needed some convincing that the students really could handle such rigorous work. "At the beginning of the year my teachers were very hesitant to trust that their kids could do more," she said. With first graders brand new to the Success Academy, "their reading levels were very low coming in without having been to our kindergarten. The teachers were unsure about what their kids were capable of and tended to err on the side of caution instead of saying, 'Wait a minute, if I give them this more challenging book, they can do it.' It wasn't until after the first eight weeks and we did our first round of assessments that they realized that the kids had grown faster than they expected." By year's end, instead of taking baby steps, her teachers were pushing even the slower children to go beyond Level J, the expected end-of-year benchmark. "They needed to see first that it really worked, but once they bought into it, they ran with it," said Michele. The story was the same at Success Academy Bronx 2.

When Danique Loving became principal of Success Academy Harlem 4 in 2010, she was surprised to learn at a kindergarten "publishing party" four weeks into the year that the teachers had instructed the five-year-olds not to write any words with the pictures they drew for their stories. "I said, 'Why not?' They had already learned at least ten sight words, and they knew all their letter sounds and letter names. I ordered journals the next day, and the kids immediately started writing in their journals." Once the teachers lifted the bar, "the kinder-gartners' writing took off because they were allowed to express themselves and no limits were put on them," said Danique, a former kindergarten teacher herself.

When Jim Manly opened Success Academy Harlem 2 he gave the eighty first graders a test to figure out where they stood on the scale that Success for All (SFA), a nationally known reading curriculum, used to assess beginning readers' skills. That first year only a dozen students "scored high enough to be on the map. Everyone else was zero or below." That meant they couldn't recognize most letters or letter blends or even ten simple sight words, much less the first reading passage, which consisted of easy sentences, such as "Sad Sam sat," Jim recalled. "Now it's literally the polar opposite with our first graders, who come in with a year of Success Academy kindergarten under their belts. At most a dozen kids score zero or below. Thirty test out of Roots because they had already begun reading in kindergarten. The remaining seventy kids were at reading levels 3 and 4, which is already ahead of schedule by SFA standards," Jim said. All but a handful had reached Level I, an aggressively rigorous first-grade reading benchmark.

That led Keri Hoyt, Success Academy's chief operating officer, to suggest that "Level I shouldn't be the standard any more. It should be Level J," Jim recounted. Now, it can be disheartening when you work hard to hit a target, only to be told immediately that that wasn't good enough. Jim remembers the feeling of frustration, but "here we are a year later and 85 to 90 percent of the kids are hitting Level J. There's something to be said for continually upping that bar," he said. "I guarantee you we'll get better because of it. None of us likes failing and probably have never failed anything significant in our lives. So we step up our game and figure it out."

Jim also encouraged three of his top teachers to pay even closer attention to how much progress their scholars were making almost on a day-by-day basis. They started giving preassessments before each new reading unit "and realized a lot of kids already knew the unit so there was no reason to teach it and they should skip to the next for these students," he said. The teachers began a friendly competition with each other to see who could move their students further the fastest and to figure out which approaches to moving kids made the biggest differences. Their colleagues also were watching the contest and learning from the results. "Hopefully it became contagious," said Jim. "We're not all the way there yet, but that frame of mind is helpful. We're going to keep doing more of this."

TAKEAWAYS

Here's our advice about rigor in a nutshell:

PRINCIPALS: Make no mistake: your teachers are going to be scared if you keep raising the bar. It takes strong, determined leadership to build a culture in which everyone—including you—is constantly asking: Is this rigorous enough? How do we know? Have the children really hit their ceiling, or are they barely off the floor?

TEACHERS: Lay aside all preconceived notions of what young children are capable of learning and doing. Be empirical. Raise the level and pick up the pace of your instruction; stop talking down to students. Let them struggle and do the hard thinking work. Get comfortable with struggling yourself to hit the heights.

PARENTS: Watch out for boredom in schools. Far too many schools do not pay attention to this, failing to ask whether or not school is interesting and rigorous enough. They have their curriculum and their teaching philosophy, and they just keep on truckin'. You need to ask yourself: Is the school aiming high enough for my child?

SCHOOL REFORMERS: Let parents, policymakers, and the public at large know the truth about how shockingly low the standards are in most states and most public schools. Raise the bar, even if the immediate results are embarrassing for teachers and painful for parents. Don't overpromise. Rigor isn't some overnight cure. It's a long slog, but it's the solution for what ails American education.

CHAPTER SIX

READING

The Starting Point for All Else

Nothing is so fundamental to a school's mission as teaching young children to read and to love reading. That it happens every day makes it no less thrilling when you see a child start to learn to read, especially *your* child—and no less depressing when you enter a school in which children heading into adolescence may be stumped by books most seven- or eight-year-olds can read.

Teaching our scholars to be great readers and writers, as THINK Literacy does, is the foundation of everything we're doing at Success Academies. THINK Literacy draws on what is called a balanced literacy approach to teaching kids to read, including reading and writing workshops, guided reading, read alouds, shared text, book discussions, and more. But THINK literacy and our approach to teaching dial things up a notch, or several notches, actually. We place an extraordinary emphasis on content over procedure. Even in kindergarten classes the children get opportunities every day to think critically about what they are reading (or being read) and to engage in freewheeling debates about the meaning of books, poems, fables, and other pieces of writing. They learn from the get-go that they can't just spout off, but rather have to cite evidence from the text to support their opinions. Even before they can read every word, our youngest scholars are turning pages and pointing to the illustrations to support their points.

Take for instance the discussion that Success Academy Bronx 1 kindergarten teacher Tara Stant orchestrated with her scholars about *Walter: The Story of a Rat* by Barbara Wersba, about an old, book-loving rat who takes up residence in the home of Amanda Pomeroy, a children's author and an irritable, lonely recluse. Walter discovers that the author has written an entire series about a secret agent mouse and that she's not quite the person portrayed on her book jackets. The teacher was reading the book to the class, frequently stopping to talk about the plot and invite the scholars to retell what was happening in their own words.

"Walter loves reading. This is just so exciting for him, living with a writer," she said. "But he's dismayed when he comes across the twenty books in her library about the feats of heroic mice."

After listening in to several children's discussions as they paired off to turn and talk, Ms. Stant said, "We've gotten in the middle of some good conversation here. We talked about betrayal. Was she trying to hurt Walter's feelings? No. She doesn't even know he's there."

"He feels discontented," Tyquan said.

"Brokenhearted and misunderstood," said Ms. Stant. "He's a rat that can read. That's pretty amazing. If Miss Pomeroy's books were all about heroic mice, why would Walter still want to read them?" she asked.

"He wants to know more about Miss Pomeroy," a girl said. Others agreed.

"Are you ready to find out what happens?" asked Ms. Stant.

"Yes," several scholars said eagerly.

"It's about to get really good," said the teacher. She resumed reading as they hung on every word. It was the point where Walter is looking at the brief biographies of the author and the illustrator on the book jacket. The blurb says that Miss Pomeroy likes to cook and garden. "But Walter knows she lives on sandwiches, and the backyard was a jungle. Now he feels a bitter taste in his mouth," said Ms. Stant. "What gave him that bitter taste? Could someone help me out here?"

"The thing that gave him the bitter taste was Miss Pomeroy because she never cooked, and when he saw her quote, it said she cooks," said Andrew.

"Maybe she's a liar," said Ms. Stant, thinking out loud, "or maybe there's another possibility: What if the book was written a long time ago?"

Andrew ran with this suggestion. "She doesn't garden and she doesn't cook any more because she's old," he said.

The discussion was in full throttle even before the first graders found out what happened. These children were learning not only how to read but also how to think for themselves and how to find evidence in the book to support their opinions. Book discussions like this are an everyday occurrence in Success Academy classrooms, even in kindergarten and first grade. Multiply this by five days a week, thirty-six weeks a year, and you get to see the power of THINK Literacy.

In this chapter we'll look at additional examples of how we turn reading classes into what Arin calls "mini English Lit seminars" for grade-schoolers.

GUIDED READING: GETTING FIRST GRADERS TO THE NEXT LEVEL

A great book discussion is the culmination of lots of other hard work on the part of our teachers that sets the children up not only to be insightful readers but also to be able to articulate and defend their ideas. Read alouds and book discussions are two of the tools in the THINK Literacy arsenal, along with shared text and guided reading. For beginning readers especially, guided reading plays a critical role in helping students learn to read and love books, while also helping them rapidly ascend reading levels.

Guided reading is the linchpin of THINK Literacy. It's the part of the day during which the teacher works with the scholars in small groups (of typically six to eight) while the rest of the class reads independently. The teacher leading the guided reading group sets the scholars up for success as together they read a challenging book, typically one level above what they can already read with ease on their own. There are three important components of a guided reading lesson.

1. *The setup*. The teacher builds excitement about the book and gives a short summary of the plot—no spoilers, but just what the kids need to know to understand the text. The teacher also points out essential vocabulary and highlights any critical or potentially confusing parts of the book that might impede comprehension. Then, most importantly, the teacher gives the scholars a "thinking job" to keep in mind as they read to help them grasp the meaning of the book.

2. *The coaching*. After distributing copies of the book, the teacher has the children read on their own, at first silently to themselves and then aloud when the teacher comes around to coach them individually. The teacher moves from scholar to scholar, and engages in rapid-fire coaching as they read, offering corrections and encouragement, and sometimes showing them how great readers tackle getting at meaning.

3. *The wrap-up*. The teacher calls the scholars back together for a book talk or discussion. The teacher closes the deal with a series of questions meant to let the kids do the thinking work and set them up to understand the meaning of the book.

Here is how Arin guided eight first graders through *Allie's Basketball Dream,* a Level K book.

"Scholars, I chose this book *Allie's Basketball Dream* by Barb Barber just for you because I know that something you've been talking a lot about in your book talks is the extent to which characters are influenced or choose not to be influenced by what other people think. This book is going to help us think even more deeply about that idea," she told them.

Allie, the main character, "is a little girl who is absolutely obsessed with becoming a professional basketball player. It's her mission in life," said Arin. "But there are all these people telling her she's not cut out to be a basketball player because she's a girl. Isn't that ridiculous?" said Arin. The children nodded and chorused yes.

"We'll have to read to find out whether Allie's influenced by these voices or whether she sticks to her dream," said Arin, pulling out a whiteboard. "Speaking of the word *dream,* there's a word you need to know to understand this book, and that word is *dream*. It is really important to the story." Writing the word down, she said, "Of course we know what a dream is, as in a dream that you have at night when you're asleep. But the word *dream* is used a bit differently in this book" to mean an aspiration or goal.

Now came the coaching. The first boy, Taj, read slowly as Arin hovered beside him: "Allie-loves-the-sound-her-new-basketball-made-as-she-bounced-it-on-the-sidewalk."

"Stop here a minute. What are you picturing as you read this part?" she asked.

"I'm picturing the firehouse and Allie bouncing the ball," Taj replied.

"Can you hear it bounce, bounce, bounce as she approached the park?" said Arin, thumping the desk three times.

"Yes," said Taj, enthusiastically adding three thumps of his own.

"How do you think she's feeling as she approaches the park with her new basketball?"

"She's feeling excited—"

"Why?"

"Because she gets to try out her new basketball."

"Yes, she's getting more excited the closer she gets. Excellent. Keep reading," said Arin.

The second child, Hakim, was a more fluid reader. "So, Hakim, you're pretty far in this story. What have you noticed about Allie's reaction to all those people who tell her in various ways that she can't play basketball?" Arin asked. "Is she listening to them? Is she stopping?"

"No, she's ignoring them," Hakim said.

"She's ignoring them?"

"She can't hear them."

"She literally cannot hear them, or she's tuning them out?"

"She's tuning them out," he replied.

"Why do you think she's doing that?"

"I think she's doing that because, because it doesn't matter if you're a girl. You can still play basketball," he said confidently.

Arin finished the coaching and, calling all eight scholars back together for the wrap-up, asked again how Allie reacted to the naysayers.

"Allie was ignoring them," said Fatimata.

"She was *ignoring* them," said Arin. Two scholars opened their books and pointed out two different pages where this was happening.

By the book's end, Allie is a basketball phenomenon being cheered on by everybody for her exploits on the hardwood. "So what's the meaning of this book? What does this book teach us?" Arin asked.

"This book teaches us that you, that if someone is laughing at you, you just ignore them and keep on doing the thing that you were doing," Hakim replied. The first graders now knew *Allie's Basketball Dream* from the inside out and understood the import of its message for their own lives.

"Scholars, that was some excellent thinking. I can tell you really understand the meaning of this book. I want you to keep it in your book bag, and you'll keep it and you'll read it throughout the week and think more deeply about it. Nice work," said Arin.

Guided Reading, Level K (First Grade) Clip 8

This clip shows the three parts of a guided reading lesson: (1) the book introduction, (2) independent reading of the book with coaching, and (3) the wrap-up. Notice the intellectual preparation required for the teacher to **close the deal** in the wrap-up. It includes understanding the book, coming up with a thinking job that will set kids up to understand the book, knowing what it will sound like to close the meaning deal, and creating a road map of questions for the wrap-up that will take kids there.

During a forty-five-minute independent reading block, the teacher will pull two or three small groups of students for guided reading. We can do this because we have trained teachers to have independent reading going on at a high level. So while the teacher is working with six or more students, the remaining twenty-two or so are silently reading books of their choice that are on their exact reading level. In the small group, the teacher helps scholars tackle a book that, like *Allie's Basketball Dream,* is slightly above what they could read on their own. It is through this guided practice that the children can become comfortable reading progressively harder books by themselves. This frequent and intense small-group instruction with a laser-like focus on acquiring the meaning of the book is a powerful tool for reading instruction. Kids love the individualized attention they get. Teachers love it because they get to know their kids as readers and help them rapidly climb reading levels to the point where they can read books of increasing depth and sophistication on their own. When done at a high level, guided reading is a phenomenal tool for helping kids become better readers. We conduct guided reading every day at Success Academies. It's a powerful way to turn children into great, insightful readers, which will propel them forward throughout life.

Clip 9   **Coaching During Guided Reading (Levels E, H, and K)**

This clip shows the critical coaching portion of a guided reading lesson at a range of levels. Notice how each teacher coaches based on what kids say and do as they are reading. If comprehension is weak, the teacher coaches there. If the reading is choppy, the teacher coaches for fluency. If kids skip over or misread unfamiliar words, the teacher coaches them to use meaning, structure, and visual cues to "word solve." As you watch this video a second time, think about the different examples of coaching. Also, see how each teacher's deep knowledge of the book is critical for effective coaching.

A guided reading alternative for advanced readers is *book clubs,* the goal of which is to deepen scholars' comprehension of books at their current reading level.

Book Club, Fourth Grade Clip 10

In this video clip we see Andrea Klein, a fourth-grade teacher at Success Academy Harlem 1 and now a member of the THINK Literacy team, introducing a new book to a group of fourth-grade scholars at Success Academy Harlem 1. When taken outside of the reading workshop unit, book clubs are a great guided reading alternative for advanced readers. The purpose of book clubs is to deepen comprehension at kids' existing independent reading levels. After introducing the book, Mrs. Klein reviews a few words scholars must comprehend to understand the book. Then she gives scholars a series of questions to which they will respond in writing after reading. **Notice that Mrs. Klein has done the intellectual work of identifying great questions that will get kids to think critically.** She also gives scholars the job of coming up with their own questions that will spark some debate within the group. Pay attention to how the teacher has clearly set the expectation that scholars in the book club will push each other to ground their ideas in evidence from the book.

CONCENTRATING ON INTELLECTUAL SPARK, NOT STRATEGIES

From kindergarten forward, THINK Literacy stresses critical thinking. It builds on standard balanced literacy components—reading and writing workshops, shared writing, interactive writing, read alouds, and book discussions—without drumming abstruse strategies into kids' heads by asking them constantly to make an inference, "contextualize" what they're reading, make predictions or "self-to-text connections," and jump through other hoops. At far too many schools the overwhelming emphasis is on imparting procedures and skills, not on helping kids fall in love with books. In other schools we'd visit, we'd hear teachers telling students four ways to make an inference or three kinds of predictions or six strategies for synthesizing, as if that were the E-ZPass lane to fluent reading. But from what we saw the teachers had no idea of what use these procedures actually were, and they had little to say if you asked them to elaborate on the meaning of the book. In too many classrooms, meaning takes a backseat to mind-numbing procedures. THINK Literacy's approach is the opposite. Skills are necessary, but they are a means to an end, not the end goal. We believe our obligation is to teach kids to think and to give them abundant practice in class at doing that. Understanding the mechanics of reading is not enough. We want them to love reading, read books by the barrel, understand books at a deep level, and be able to communicate elegantly.

 Clip 11   **Reading Workshop Direct Instruction, Second Grade**

In this video of Jennifer Cui and her second-grade class at Success Academy Harlem 4, we see one brief lesson within the context of a larger unit that focuses on character study in fiction. Reading workshop lessons follow a predictable structure that allows them to be fast (ten minutes or less) and effective. The brevity of direct instruction ensures ample time for independent reading and practice. First, Ms. Cui tells her scholars what they will be learning that day and *why* it's important. Infusing purpose makes the lesson authentic. Otherwise it's merely an exercise. Next, Ms. Cui models the **teaching point**. She does so using a book scholars know well, allowing her to focus on just an excerpt that illuminates *why* this teaching point is useful. Ms. Cui has anticipated that her scholars may struggle with going beyond a surface interpretation of character actions, so she models getting into and out of a similar struggle by rereading and pushing her own thinking to the next level. Next, Ms. Cui gives scholars the opportunity to quickly try out the teaching point on their own as she **checks for understanding** and coaches. Notice how she quickly gives the class an example of a student who is pushing beyond the surface to drive this point home. Finally, Ms. Cui names the teaching point once more, reminding scholars *why* using this tactic will help them be better readers.

How much do our scholars love to read and be read to?

Late one afternoon in Kelly Ortagus's kindergarten class at Success Academy Harlem 5, a mother was conspicuously arranging decorations and cutting the cake for the class party celebrating her daughter's sixth birthday.

But all eyes were glued to Ms. Ortagus as she read, at their request, another *Skippyjon Jones* book by Judy Schachner about an adventurous, big-eared kitten that looks like a chihuahua.

"How'd I know you were going to pick this one?" she said, a trifle ruefully. "*Skippyjon Jones in Mummy Trouble,* by Judy Schachner. 'Skippyjon Jones did his best thinking outside of the box. And this twisted his Momma's whiskers tighter than a Texas tornado . . .'" The children tittered as she gave an actor's intonation to the lines of each new character.

"'HUH!' mused Momma. '*The Curse of the Cat Mummy?* Hmmmm. Why this will give you nightmares, boy, with an upset tummy, too. Plus a puppytale on the grandest scale. This story is taboo,'" she read.

"Ohhhh," said several scholars.

"You know what 'taboo' meant?"

"Yes," Destiny said. "You can't read it."

"It's not just that you can't read it. It's off-limits," said Ms. Ortagus.

"You can't look at it," Destiny agreed.

"You can't look at it, can't see it, can't hear about it, can't talk about it. Taboo," said Ms. Ortagus. "But Skippyjon Jones was in no mood to listen to his momma. So he skedaddled into his room."

"Skedaddled," repeated Invi. "What's that?"

"Skedaddled," repeated Ms. Ortagus. "What do you think skedaddled means? What does it sound like, Joan?"

"Like skipping fast," Joan replied.

The read aloud went on without so much as a glance back at the birthday cake. It wasn't difficult to understand why. Ms. Ortagus was not just tickling their funny bone, she was firing their imagination.

It's a far cry from going into a classroom and watching a teacher almost literally check the items off a skills checklist. What we want to see, and what we do see, is the teacher throwing off intellectual sparks that inspire the children and ignite their passion. Up to three hours of class time each day devoted to reading and writing sounds like a lot, and it is, but it often goes by too quickly for our hungry scholars. It gives our teachers plenty of time to model their own reading and writing, and to provide individual coaching. We're certain that the more students read now, the greater the chance they will become voracious, lifelong readers—and a child who loves reading and reads exceptionally well can teach herself or himself anything.

Clip 12 **Eduspeak Versus English**

The first segment shows a common mistake many teachers and school leaders make: they let skills and strategies overwhelm *thinking*. As we see in this part of the clip, a hyperfocus on skills and strategies obscures rather than illuminates meaning. As you watch the second segment, notice how the teacher's focus as he thinks aloud is squarely on meaning, not on naming fancy skills and strategies, and how this exponentially increases student understanding.

Straight through middle school we devote an enormous amount of class time to nothing but reading. Outside visitors to Success Academies sometimes remark on how surprised they are to find scholars curled up on a beanbag chair or lying on the reading carpet or sitting at their desk, deeply immersed in books for long stretches of time without any "actual" teaching going on (apart from small-group instruction). Our classrooms, filled to the brim with great books, take on the ambience of a library. Any doubts the visitors may harbor are removed once they hear a riveting book discussion.

Our reading curriculum evolved into THINK Literacy over several years. When we opened the first Success Academy Harlem in August 2006 with kindergarten and first-grade classes, we used the highly scripted Success for All curriculum developed by Robert Slavin, director of the Center for Research and Reform in Education at Johns Hopkins University, Nancy Madden, and their Johns Hopkins colleagues. Success for All was geared toward disadvantaged children. It's been adopted by many urban schools and districts. We still use its Reading Roots books to teach phonics in kindergarten and first grade. But academically our scholars are advantaged, not disadvantaged. "Success for All wasn't enough. The kids did not read nearly enough. The books were not sufficiently challenging. It is skills based. It is not about the meaning of books. The emphasis is on skills, not critical thinking," said Carrie Roby, principal of Success Academy Upper West and one of our original second-grade teachers.

So instead of setting out with remediation as our starting point, we began with the goal of turning our classrooms into magical places piled high with great books, places where children get the intellectual nourishment to make their dreams come true. And we helped our teachers understand that it isn't enough for the children to be reading the books thoroughly. Teachers had to pore over the books beforehand and be ready to ask penetrating questions while still letting the children do the thinking work for themselves, as they did in Tara Stant's class with *Walter* and in Kelly Ortagus's class with the almost insufferable (for adults!) *Skippyjon Jones*.

We spend weeks each summer training new teachers, placing special emphasis on their role in teaching THINK Literacy at a high level and on being thoroughly prepared to lead invigorating book discussions in the classroom. Before they ask students to do the hard-thinking work, the teachers themselves must study the books, poems, fables, and other stories they assign as hard as they studied works of literature in college. It takes painstaking efforts to inspire teachers to take on this profound responsibility of truly understanding the books they teach. "Do not assume you understand either the point of a lesson or a kid's book without closely studying it," Eva told 150 new teachers at Teacher Success Academy, or T school, in July 2011. "You may say, 'How much could there be to a Dr. Seuss story?' He's actually a very sophisticated author. There's a lot to get out of his books, and if you don't understand that, you will not be well prepared."

"The biggest mistake you as teachers can make is to read a page or a book quickly and say, 'I got it!' when actually you haven't gotten it," Eva said. "If a lesson were that simple, then it probably doesn't need to be taught to the kids. You yourself have to struggle to make sure you understand it at an adult level and then decide how to teach it to kids." Likewise, Paola Zalkind, a leadership resident at Success Academy Harlem 2 and former kindergarten and third-grade teacher, counsels new teachers not to assume that even beginning readers and picture books lack depth and are a piece of cake to teach. "Our richest, deepest conversations and some of our biggest debates have been over the meaning of first-grade books we read," she said.

In the remainder of this chapter, let's take a closer look at examples of the riveting classroom debates we're talking about with books from different genres—from fables and fairy tales to biographies and magical fiction.

POSING THOUGHT-PROVOKING QUESTIONS

We take special pains to choose books that intrigue students, pose ethical dilemmas, and force them to think hard about important issues. But a great teacher knows how to get a good discussion going even around stories that aren't candidates for the *Norton Anthology of Literature*. We observed one kindergarten class at Success Academy Bronx 2 in which the teacher had just read Amy Hest's

Jamaica Louise James to the class, a book about eight-year-old Jamaica, whose grandmother is a token collector in the subway (this was before MetroCards) and regales Jamaica each night with stories about her customers. As a birthday surprise for Grammy, Jamaica draws pictures of these characters and, with her mother's help, tapes them up on the subway station walls. The commuters are delighted to recognize their own likenesses in the child's hand.

"Why was Jamaica's idea so great? How did it make the subway a better place?" teacher Andrew Vidockler asked his two dozen kindergartners.

"It made her grandmother happy," said Janelle.

"It sounds to me like Jamaica made a difference in her community. How can we make a difference in our community?" the teacher asked.

"We could go to the subway and paint paintings on the wall," a boy replied.

The conversation already showed signs of stagnation. Eva jumped in to try to steer it in a new direction. "Is making one's community better always the best thing?" she asked. "For instance, is the school principal better than someone who just takes care of her family and pays her taxes?" she queried. The scholars had difficulty deciding.

Mr. Vidockler brought the discussion closer to home. "Can I put it another way? What if Jamaica hadn't done her homework that night? Is that a good choice? Isn't making a better community more important?" he asked. Now the scholars were divided almost down the middle. Some thought Jamaica did the right thing, even if she skipped her homework, but one boy warned of the consequences: "If you don't do your homework, you can get in trouble."

Mr. Vidockler said his own parents run a business "and have to go to work every day. On Sunday they volunteer at the hospital. If they just went and did community work every single day and didn't take care of their responsibilities, what would happen, Frederico?"

"They would be fired," said Frederico. The debate went on, not restricted to the bare facts of what Jamaica did in the story, but starting to grapple with the implications of the choices one makes in life.

In the hands of a well-trained teacher who has done his or her homework, even the simplest of children's books can lend themselves to great debates. In a kindergarten class down the hall, the teacher read aloud and orchestrated a discussion of *Down the Road* by Alice Schertle, which tells the story of the first time a young girl named Hetty is allowed to go to town by herself to buy eggs. Ignoring instructions to return home straightaway, Hetty stops to climb a tree to pick an apple and winds up breaking all the eggs. Now she is afraid to go home. But her forgiving parents find her in the orchard, pick and eat some apples themselves, and then bring home more so they can make apple pie instead of eggs for breakfast.

Does Hetty deserve such a happy ending? Hardly, but even when a story sends the wrong message, it doesn't mean the class debate has to miss the mark.

"Why weren't Hetty's parents angry with her?" the teacher asked.

"They wanted apples, too," a scholar, Elijah, responded. Like most of his classmates, he seemed willing to give Hetty a pass for her conduct.

Arin spoke up. "I disagree with all of you. Her only job was to get the eggs. I don't understand why her parents were so forgiving. If it were my child, I'd give her a time-out. Do you think I am right?" she asked.

"But she was very careful," Damien said in defense of Hetty.

"I don't care if she was careful. She still broke the eggs," said Arin. "If I was being careful but stepped on a few scholars' fingers, wouldn't that matter? Are you saying it only matters what you mean to do?" These five- and six-year-olds were being asked to confront ethical dilemmas, not just follow the words of a simple children's story. The book talk was taking these kindergartners a lot farther "down the road" than perhaps even the author envisioned.

TURNING KINDERGARTNERS INTO READERS

Even before the children can read and write fluently on their own, they begin learning through THINK Literacy how to become great readers in their own right. We employ a technique called emergent storybook reading, based on the research of professor Elizabeth Sulzby, to do this in kindergarten classes like the one that Kelsey Contreras, now part of the network literacy team, taught using a book version of the Norwegian fairy tale "Three Billy Goats Gruff." She'd read this book and others to the class multiple times so they were very familiar with the story, and then had shown them how to "read" these books with partners (not decoding but retelling the stories based on their familiarity with them), acting them out with gestures and story language from the book. Emergent storybook reading lets kids get a handle on meaning and story structure so they are primed and ready for print when independent reading and guided reading begin in October.

"In addition, I do Fairy Tale Fridays, telling them a tale orally without holding a book. It helps them imagine the story and practice and get exposure to the art of storytelling," said Ms. Contreras. "The kids love it. When I have to cancel Fairy Tale Fridays, some kids cry, they love reading and listening to the stories so much. That's our goal. Eventually we want them to love reading on their own so much they cry when we tell them they have to put the book down," she said.

On this morning she was getting the scholars to do their own boisterous versions of the billy goats and the troll beneath the bridge. Ms. Contreras, a theater and English major in college, showed them how. "What's happening in the story? The mean, ugly, ferocious troll," she harrumphed, "just threatened to gobble up"—and here she dropped her voice to a squeak—"the tiny little billy goat." The children smiled and laughed as she read the littlest billy goat's lines in a quivering falsetto. She instructed them to practice on each other the voice of the grumpy troll and the wily big goat, and then praised their enthusiastic renditions. "It's something that they sort of innately have in them," she said afterward, and it's a sure way to increase both comprehension and enthusiasm for reading.

Clip 13   Emergent Storybook Practice Group, Kindergarten

In this reading practice group within the emergent storybook unit, Ms. Contreras has pulled six kindergarten scholars together based on a common need: although they are remembering the stories in their emergent storybooks, Ms. Contreras wants to deepen their understanding by having them use gestures to act out key points in each book as they read and story-tell. As she tells the six five-year-olds in front of her, this will have the added benefit of making their storytelling infinitely more engaging for their audience (their classmates). As you watch this practice group, notice the considerable ground Ms. Contreras is able to cover in five short minutes. First, she tells the scholars what they are practicing and why. Next, they try it together. Finally, the scholars say the teaching point on their own, while Ms. Contreras coaches and **checks for understanding**. This last part is critical because it allows the teacher to assess the efficacy of her own teaching in real time and tells her whether she has **closed the deal.** Whereas some scholars in the group may have achieved mastery around the teaching point, others will need to be pulled tomorrow for another bite at the apple.

Emergent Storybook Direct Instruction, Kindergarten   Clip 14

In this reading lesson within the emergent storybook unit, Ms. Contreras teaches her kindergarten class to read dialogue just like the characters would deliver it by taking into account what's happening at that point in the story and how the characters probably feel about these events. Thus, before most are able to read conventionally, these five-year-olds will understand what dialogue is, how to read it expressively, and how doing so deepens one's understanding of the story. As you watch this video, you are likely to notice the incredible **joy** with which Ms. Contreras and her scholars approach reading. She knows that this is her chance to hook them on reading, and she uses every second of her lesson to do so. Also watch for indicators that Ms. Contreras is **intellectually prepared at a high level.** How can you tell that she understands the purpose of the lesson? Why has she chosen *these specific parts* of the book to model and to have scholars practice? Where has she built in **checks for understanding** of the teaching point?

From Fairy Tale Fridays and lessons like these, our young scholars are learning how to bring words to life, and that's an ability that will serve them well long after they have forgotten the moral of "Three Billy Goats Gruff."

PUTTING ONESELF INTO RUBY BRIDGES'S SHOES

THINK Literacy teaches children how to put themselves into the shoes of characters from real life, too. Carrie Roby did this memorably in a reading practice group at Success Academy Harlem 1 with a small number of third-grade scholars who were reading *Through My Eyes,* Ruby Bridges's real-life account of her experiences as a six-year-old being escorted through a mob by federal marshals to integrate the William Frantz Public School in New Orleans in 1960. Ruby knew nothing of the controversy over desegregation and actually mistook the jostling, shouting crowd for a Mardi Gras parade. Looking up at the handsome school building, so different from the run-down, segregated school she attended for kindergarten, she thought to herself it must be a college. Norman Rockwell later drew a famous painting called *The Problem We All Live With,* which was inspired by those images of little Ruby Bridges walking to school in her white dress and Mary Janes, surrounded and protected by the four U.S. marshals, seen only from their broad shoulders down (John Steinbeck, driving through New Orleans that morning, witnessed the mob scene and wrote caustically about it in *Travels with Charley*).

Ms. Roby told the six third graders in her reading practice group something she'd noticed: that when they read books with characters whose lives are similar to their own, "you're able to understand them pretty well. But as we've been reading more difficult texts like biographies and historical fiction, you're able to understand what's happening, but it's not as easy for us to understand those characters."

"What I want to practice with you here today is how to experience the story from the perspective of the main character by stepping into her shoes," she said. "That means that we're really going to become that character . . . It's going to help you understand your character and your book at a much deeper level."

The scholars began describing their own feelings as they made that walk on that turbulent morning. Despite the shouts and noise, Ruby isn't quivering. She's thinking this new school looks so much more impressive than her own.

"I feel happier because I'm in a good and better place than my own school," said Kasiya.

"It made her feel like she was in college," said Kayla.

"That's really interesting," said Ms. Roby. "If you read this book and weren't thinking very deeply and carefully, you might think, oh, Ruby Bridges is just scared. She's this little girl, and people are yelling and throwing things. But you scholars are getting into her shoes. You're experiencing this from her perspective."

Reading Practice Group, Third Grade Clip 15

In this video we see Ms. Roby, then a second-grade teacher at Success Academy Harlem 1, facilitating a reading practice group made up of third-grade scholars. Something we've long admired about Ms. Roby's teaching is that she conveys her high expectations for kids **simply by talking to them like she knows they are smart.** There is no singsong voice, no alternate teacher persona, just great books and a passion for them shared by teacher and scholars. As you watch this video, notice how Ms. Roby makes sure scholars know exactly what she's pulled them to the rug to practice, and why it's important. Notice also how Ms. Roby **checks for scholar understanding** at every step of the way, through cold calling and coaching, and **presses** scholars to use the teaching point to understand the book more deeply. As a result, Xavian is able to "see the marshals around [him] and hear people screaming," leading him to the conclusion that *inside Ruby Bridges's shoes* people hate him, but he is not going to hate them. Finally, notice how after kids try out the teaching point on their own, Ms. Roby sends them off individually to continue reading **as soon as they've mastered what she's taught them.** She does this to convey the urgency of independent reading time.

From start to finish, this all took place quickly, which is just how we want it. A reading practice group like this is "down and dirty. It doesn't take that long. The point is to get them back to their reading because kids ultimately get better at reading by reading, not by listening to me talk about books and strategies," said Ms. Roby, now principal of Success Academy Upper West.

STORIES THAT HIT CLOSE TO HOME

Stories that hit close to home, that address conflicts or longings in our students' lives, fit well with the THINK Literacy approach. The book *Those Shoes* by Maribeth Boelts can work for that reason for children from kindergarten up to third grade. It's the story of a boy named Jeremy who is desperate for a pair of the expensive, high-top sneakers other kids wear, but denied by a grandmother who says they can't afford it. Adding insult to injury, when his old shoes fall apart in school, the guidance counselor gives him hand-me-down Velcro sneakers with a cartoon character on the side. Jeremy finds a pair of the coveted sneakers in a thrift shop and buys them even though they are too small. Eventually he gives them away to a classmate also in desperate need of shoes and makes a friend in the bargain.

Courtney Olsen read and discussed the book with her third graders at Success Academy Harlem 2. Ms. Olsen, now a leadership resident, said beforehand that part of her preparation was "being totally prepared with really deep and sometimes controversial or provocative questions that allow the scholars to think about things in a different way." She also tried to give the scholars ownership of the whole-class conversation because they "learn so much more when they're doing the talking and they're building on each other's ideas."

She started by reading the book aloud, doing her first think aloud at the point where Jeremy is getting the second-hand shoes from the counselor, Mr. Alfrey.

"So, I'm Jeremy right now, and I have to put on those silly, Tweety Bird shoes. I can just feel my cheeks burning. I'm thinking about how humiliating and mortifying it's going to be to go back into class with all of my judgmental peers. Not only will they know that I have to wear these stupid shoes, but they are going to know that I can't afford the other ones," Ms. Olsen said. Back in class, Jeremy tries not to cry, but when he's writing his spelling words, "every word looks like the word 'shoes' and my grip on my pencil is so tight I think it might bust," she read. She asked the scholars to grip their own pencils tightly and turn to a partner to talk about their thoughts and emotions.

Ms. Olsen roamed the room and listened in on what the pairs were saying, then called for scholars' attention again and repeated some of what she heard about how mad and angry Jeremy was, with the tension and frustration inside him about to burst like a volcano.

They resumed reading the story, from the part in which Jeremy wastes his grandmother's money on the thrift shop sneakers that don't fit to the point where he gives them away to a classmate even less fortunate than himself. "How is it possible," Ms. Olsen asked, "for the story to have an upbeat ending when Jeremy doesn't actually get what he wants?"

"When he gave Antonio those shoes, he actually made a friend, and I think friends are more important than shoes," said Shane. He pointed out that Jeremy did wind up on a snowy day with the new winter boots his grandmother had been saving for. But others said Jeremy still probably wanted those high-top sneakers, too.

Although the debate didn't produce a definitive answer to the teacher's question, the students clearly had moved beyond a surface understanding of the book, Ms. Olsen said afterward. Next "they need to learn to not just agree or disagree but to start asking each other questions about their ideas and keep the conversation going."

"I'm working on really giving the kids ownership during the book discussion," she added. "The scholars learn so much more when they are doing the talking and they're building on each other's ideas."

High-Level Think Aloud Versus Low-Level Think Aloud   Clip 16

In the first segment of this clip the teacher uses her think aloud simply to explain the book, telling scholars that the character is embarrassed. The problem with this is that because kids are smart (even though they're short!) they already knew the character is embarrassed. This think aloud does little to nothing to reveal behind the curtain what excellent readers do. In the second segment the teacher goes beyond the surface-level idea that the character is embarrassed to discover, by putting herself in Jeremy's shoes, that his cheeks are *burning* with shame as he imagines his friends' reactions to his Tweety Bird shoes. This think aloud not only advances kids' understanding of the book but also shows them that great readers connect to what they're reading by thinking and feeling as if they *are* the character.

We encourage our teachers to wrap up the book debate with a high-level summary of the scholars' ideas, but not to let it drag on if it wanders off course. Sometimes it's better just to cut your losses and to keep the conversation brisk. After all, with THINK Literacy's extended reading classes, the teachers and the scholars will get another chance tomorrow to knock the book discussion out of the park.

Rising to the Reading Challenges

We're strict constructionists when it comes to reading. The text is king. We expect close reading. We tell our teachers and students that they should pore over every poem, story, fable, biography, and other piece of writing at least three times:

1. Once for pleasure

2. A second time to determine the meaning

3. A third time to understand exactly how the author conveys this meaning

We also preach constantly about the importance of having students cite evidence from the text to support their opinions. "This notion of evidence is critical," Eva told new teachers at the summer training and orientation sessions at T school. "You don't get to have opinions without evidence. No one is going to believe you. I'm right just because I stomp my foot? No, you've got to marshal evidence to convince your audience you know what you're talking about. We're obsessed with everybody all the way down marshaling evidence."

We stress the importance of using books and stories that pose genuine ethical dilemmas to children instead of just giving them bromides. "I hate it when I go into a school and the kids are saying, 'Racism is bad. This book teaches you that racism is bad.' Of course racism is bad. The kids knew that before they came to school," Eva told the new teachers.

GETTING THE MOST OUT OF *MAGNUS MAXIMUS*

Great books lend themselves to great discussions. One is *Magnus Maximus, a Marvelous Measurer* by Kathleen Pelley, a lushly illustrated tale about an eccentric scientist living in a seaside, Victorian town who is so consumed with his measurements and instruments that he is oblivious to the world around him. He measures almost everything, including fabulous things like the itchiness of an itch and the stinkiness of socks. When Magnus gets a runaway circus lion to stand still while he measures its whiskers and the fleas in its mane, the grateful townspeople build a statue in his honor. But the single-minded Magnus is oblivious to friends' joys, sorrows, and concerns. His view of the world changes one day when he breaks his thick glasses and encounters a young boy by the strand. The boy extends a hand, and Magnus initially thinks he wants it measured. When the boy explains he wants to play together, Magnus says, "Oh, now I see." They frolic in the surf and build a sand castle before parting. Magnus gets new glasses the next day, along with a new outlook. He still takes lots of measurements, but at day's end repairs to his garden with a pot of tea and a plate of sardine sandwiches to watch the sun set, the moon swell, and stars sparkle in the endless sky.

We used this book to train our principals. At Success Academies, the only thing more important than teacher training is principal training, because principals are the ones who train and inspire the teachers. Every year principals undergo eight weeks of training, which starts over the summer. During the school year, this training comes in the form of Leader Study Groups. The emphasis is on showing principals how to move teacher practice and then actually having them do so, guiding the teachers as they work in classrooms with real kids.

On this particular day we took on how to really understand a first-grade book, how to run a successful planning meeting around the meaning of the book, and then how to teach that meaning to kids while letting the children do the thinking work. It was a lot to squeeze into two hours, but remember, we all believe in and practice *fast*.

So the goal for this critical training session was to orchestrate a penetrating discussion of *Magnus Maximus* before the principals would coach teachers on the book. As we always do, we asked them to think of "premortems"—the things the teachers might say or do wrong. Arin asked what a teacher who hadn't spent much time with the book would say was the main idea.

"Pay more attention to nice things in life," one principal responded.

"And he shouldn't work so hard," said another, evoking laughs from our workaholic leaders.

But "what's the deepest level of meaning?" Arin pressed. Eva noted that the classroom teachers have a lot on their plates, with "multiple lessons to plan. They read the book on a Sunday night, and they are teaching it on Wednesday. What possible misconceptions are going to roll off their tongues?"

"The typical clichés—stop and smell the roses," said one principal. "It's not incorrect, but it's not as precise as it might be." Several others took stabs, all talking about the need to balance work and pleasure. "That is certainly right. But what else can we say to enrich that?" Eva pushed them further.

The encounter on the beach with the boy "is big," said one principal. "Obviously the glasses breaking is symbolic," said another, as was Magnus's "Oh, now I see" comment when he took the boy's outstretched hand. (Arin mentioned that a first grader in a class in which she taught *Magnus Maximus* had observed that without his glasses, Magnus "can see fun.")

"I'm sure everyone could come up with more," said Eva, who then asked Jim Manly, principal of Success Academy Harlem 2, to read the review we had prepared in advance.

> *The alliterative title* Magnus Maximus, a Marvelous Measurer *suggests the whimsical tale within about an obsessive measurer. This unique picture book tells the story of an old man who is compelled to measure things, not just ordinary things, but all kinds of things, like the wobbliness of jellyfish or the itchiness of an itch . . . [In the end] the exuberant picture of the old and the young splashing in the waves conveys their joy and found friendship. This experience transforms Maximus, and he realizes there is more to life than measuring. He comes to understand that his obsession with measuring had prevented him from seeing the many joys of life. The boy's outstretched hand teaches the old man to open his eyes to the beauty of nature, friendship, and such simple pleasures as splashing in the ocean.*

There was a nervous, collective laugh when we asked the principals to talk about the differences between this elegant interpretation of the story and their own. For starters, it conveyed so many more details, they agreed. The principals then began batting ideas back and forth about how to teach the story, citing different passages and pointing to illustrations that conveyed Magnus's obsession, his loneliness, and his eventual change of heart.

"What we're uncovering here," said Eva, "is that it's not enough to understand the thesis of the book. To really understand it, we've got to understand how all the little parts and details are put together to create and support that thesis. And we've got to lead kids there, too." Arin said no one would dispute that "you can't teach people to understand biology or physics or calculus if you yourself have not mastered the content. We need to convey to our teachers that 'understanding the books is your calculus, your physics. This is what you need to master.'"

There was new vigor in the room when the principals sat down to coach first-grade teachers on preparing to teach *Magnus Maximus*.

WHAT MAKES MAGNUS MAXIMUS HAPPY?

Magnus Maximus is now a staple of our reading list for first graders. A few weeks after this Leader Study Group convened, Michele Caracappa, principal of Success Academy Bronx 1, was reading the book to rapt first graders. She paused at strategic points in the story to think aloud and to ask the scholars to turn to a partner and discuss events and ideas as they unfolded.

In this video we see Ms. Caracappa, founding teacher and principal of Success Academy Bronx 1, model a read aloud for her teachers in a first-grade class. First, notice that Ms. Caracappa has picked a world-class book. We believe that the quality of the books we read to kids matters enormously, and just by choosing this great book, *Magnus Maximus, a Marvelous Measurer,* Ms. Caracappa has **upped the level of rigor.** As you watch this video, notice the following indicators that Ms. Caracappa has done her **intellectual preparation at a high level:**

- She knows and understands the book inside and out. She uses both the text and illustrations to develop her ideas in front of scholars during think alouds.

- She has strategically chosen places in the book to think aloud and have kids turn and talk that will set them up to understand the meaning of the book. For example, she knows that kids need to understand that Magnus's bravery in approaching the lion really masks his blind obsession for measuring. So she prompts her students to discuss whether it's bravery or an obsession that drives Magnus.

When she finished reading, Ms. Caracappa rearranged the scholars so they were seated around the perimeter of the reading carpet and could see everyone's face as he or she spoke. "The ending seems so different to me from things we knew about Magnus in the beginning of the story. Here's my question I want you to think about: What makes Magnus truly happy?" she asked the class. "Be sure to back [your answer] up with evidence from the text."

A girl named Dakara said measuring was what made Magnus happy "because everybody is celebrating him and made a statue of him" after he tamed the lion.

A girl beside her, Chaqual, piped up, "I disagree with Dakara because actually it was the boy who made him happy. First he was measuring and measuring and measuring, and then when his glasses broke, he took a break from it." The boy, she added, made Magnus realize "you don't always have to measure. You can sometimes relax."

A third girl, Sydney, chimed in: "I think . . . both make him happy. He enjoys measuring, and he enjoys the real things in life."

"Sometimes you can do fun stuff and don't count all the time," said Alexander. A classmate, Evelynn, asked, "What's your evidence, Alexander?" Alexander cited all the fun things Magnus did with the boy after breaking his glasses.

These first graders clearly got the main idea. Afterward, discussing her role in the debate, Ms. Caracappa stressed the importance of the planning and preparation "so that I'm asking great questions that are going to key kids into the big ideas in the text," but leaving them to do the thinking work. "I want to make sure I'm not just feeding it to them, but rather that they are truly grappling with the big ideas in the text, and they are the ones who are truly sharing their ideas and coming up with the evidence to support those ideas," she said.

 Clip 18   **Book Discussion, First Grade**

As you watch Ms. Caracappa facilitate this first-grade book discussion about *Magnus Maximus,* notice how scholars automatically use evidence from the book to support their thinking. Remember that in Clip 17 Ms. Caracappa modeled this in each of her think alouds. **What moves do you see her make during this book discussion to teach kids to ground their conversation in the book?**

As you watch this book discussion, also notice how Ms. Caracappa has done the intellectual work of preparing a road map of questions. She **pitches the lesson high,** and she does not make the mistake of thinking that her first question will take scholars a long time to answer. Rather she has prepared a follow-up question, and another, and another, all driving toward the main idea of the book. Having this **road map of great questions** frees Ms. Caracappa up to listen to kids, and to reference the book based on their ideas. As we've seen in other book discussions, Ms. Caracappa acts as a facilitator, **letting kids do the intellectual heavy lifting.**

THE TIGER RISING ENGAGES FOURTH GRADERS' IMAGINATION

If *Magnus Maximus* is great for stimulating book discussions in first grade, it's hard to miss with *The Tiger Rising* in fourth grade. This 125-page novel by Kate DiCamillo falls into a category of fiction that is often called magical realism. It's about twelve-year-old Rob Horton's discovery of a caged tiger in the woods near the Florida motel where he and his father moved after the death of Rob's mother from cancer six months earlier. Rob suffers in silence the torments of bullies on the school bus. Self-inflicted scratches and a rash on his legs are visible signs of how he has bottled up his feelings since the loss of his mother. Rob shares the secret of the tiger with another newcomer to the school, the feisty Sistene Bailey, who has her own troubles but stands up to the bullies. Together they wrestle with whether to set the tiger free, and then with the consequences of their actions.

Andrea Klein, then teaching fourth grade at Success Academy Harlem 1, had read the book aloud with her class over multiple days and facilitated several discussions. For this final conversation, after reading aloud the last chapter, she posed the biggest question of all: "Is the tiger real or a figment of Rob's imagination?" It drew a torrent of responses.

"Figurative," said Aiyisha, citing a passage in which Rob imagined that he had stuffed all his feelings into a suitcase like the one he packed when they moved from Jacksonville after his mother's funeral. When Mr. Horton shot the tiger, Aiyisha said, it symbolized Rob's need to open that suitcase up and express his feelings to his dad.

Kiana agreed, and said that "when Rob and Sistene set the tiger free, it was like Rob setting his sadness free . . . and letting the happiness come out." But others disagreed with equal vehemence. "The tiger is real because if it was his imagination, the dad couldn't have killed it and Sistene couldn't have [seen] it," insisted a third student.

The debate raged back and forth, with Mrs. Klein never making a definitive pronouncement of who was right and who was wrong, but giving her students every opportunity to take ownership of their own strong views about the challenging, intriguing text.

Debates like this were an everyday occurrence in Mrs. Klein's reading classes. Her copy of *The Tiger Rising* was stuffed with color-coded Post-it notes, making even more evident how much and how closely she had studied the book beforehand.

When a new cadre of Success Academy teachers were shown a video of Mrs. Klein's lesson at summer T School, they burst into applause afterward. They were struck by how she talked with the scholars like they were adults, and by how she slipped in elegant vocabulary without stopping to say, "This means this."

She didn't ask fact recall questions or say, "Readers, watch me. I'm synthesizing." She was just letting them in on the thinking that excellent readers do in a very real, powerful way.

Book Discussion, Fourth Grade

> In this video we see Mrs. Klein's fourth-grade class passionately debate whether the tiger in *The Tiger Rising* is real or figurative. As you watch this video, think about the steps of **intellectual preparation** Mrs. Klein took to facilitate a book discussion at this level early in the school year. Also, notice how the tone with which Mrs. Klein addresses the book and her scholars contributes to the sky-high levels of scholar investment we see in this clip.

That's exactly how THINK Literacy is supposed to work. Not every book debate is going to move in the direction the teacher hoped. That's why our approach places so much emphasis on teachers' study and preparation beforehand. They must come to each book discussion armed with not just one good question but a whole series of questions, including follow-ups if the debate takes a wrong or pointless turn—or if the first child to speak nails the answer. We want ideas in these discussions to move in rapid-fire succession, volleying back and forth in an intellectual Ping-Pong match. It's impossible to do that if the teacher asks an obvious or dead-end question that doesn't lend itself to debate.

TAKEAWAYS

PRINCIPALS: You're the instructional leaders. Excellent reading instruction is about the grown-ups' understanding precisely and thoroughly the books you are teaching. This cannot be skipped. There are no shortcuts. Principals, help your teachers get mastery of the stories, poems, fables, and other expository pieces of writing they are going to teach in class. Practice with the teachers preparing great questions to ask that will make students think. Make sure your classrooms are stocked with rich children's literature.

TEACHERS: Study, study, study. Don't assume you understand children's books and poems without reading them carefully multiple times. Give the students ample opportunities to come up with the main idea and express their opinions, but always insist that they cite evidence from the text.

PARENTS: Read constantly with your child. Ask your child to tell you in his or her own words the meaning or the point of the poems, stories, biographies, and other assigned readings, and—just like your child's teacher—ask your child to show you in the text the evidence that supports his or her ideas.

SCHOOL REFORMERS: Recognize that teaching children to be great readers—in regard to both the volume of books they read and the depth of their understanding—is paramount, and that how well educators do this depends on how much training they receive and how well they master the content. The proliferation of procedures and checklists of strategies will not fix our schools. Better-trained and well-read teachers and principals will.

CHAPTER SEVEN

WRITING

Putting Ideas into the World with Elegance

One of our first-grade classes recently went to see a performance by the Paper Bag Players, the wonderful New York City troupe that since the 1960s has been entertaining children and parents with musical theater, freewheeling dances, mime, and painting onstage with props as ordinary as cardboard boxes, craft paper, and of course paper bags.

The next morning Violet Davenport, then a founding faculty member and first-grade teacher at Success Academy Harlem 1 and now dean of students at Success Academy Harlem 3, began writing a story with the students about the experience. The kids could not get over how the performers were able to weave a highly compelling tale from such seemingly mundane objects.

Ms. Davenport asked what the main idea of their story should be.

"The big idea we want to show," said Donovan, "is that if you use your imagination the story can be fun, even if the stuff they use is boring."

"So how could we show that from beginning to end?" Ms. Davenport asked.

"We could show how at the beginning it was boring, and then we wanted to see what would happen next," Sinai offered.

"How did you feel when you first saw the guy come out on stage with a paper bag?" the teacher asked.

"We were bored," several students replied, and Ms. Davenport wrote that on the big sheet on her easel.

Arin happened to be in the classroom for a literacy observation and immediately jumped into the conversation. "What did that look like on your face and body?" she asked. The kids' answers quickly flew back.

"We were slumped in our chairs."

"We had our hands over our faces."

"We were looking away."

The teacher wrote down the pièce de résistance: "We were slumped in our chairs like wilted flowers."

"And how did they feel when the players transformed themselves into pirates on a search for buried treasure?" Ms. Davenport asked.

"Our faces lit up," one girl said.

"Like what?" the teacher asked.

"Like fireflies." And the teacher wrote that: "Our faces lit up like fireflies."

What a long way they had come, in sixty seconds, from "We were bored."

We're passionate at Success Academies about teaching children to become great writers. It starts in kindergarten, even before some of them know all their letters, much less properly spelled words. We set aside blocks of time each day for them to do nothing but write, with supervision and steady help from their teacher.

Along with reading, writing is the heart of what we do at Success Academies. It is the key that will open the doors to college and great career opportunities for our scholars. "We don't want them to look at writing as an assignment. We want them to look at it as an important part of their development that matters not just today or next week but for the rest of their lives," said Dionne Beckford, a veteran teacher and now a leadership resident at Success Academy Harlem 2.

Eva and the Writing Center at Penn

Success Academies' practice, practice, practice approach to writing reflects in no small part Eva's determination to hone her writing skills in college after being told point-blank by a professor that she didn't know how to write. She was soon a steady customer at the college writing center, and went on to become a published author. She tells the story:

> *I struggled with writing. I was an A student in a public high school renowned for science and math, but they didn't teach us to write. At Penn it was quickly evident that the kids who went to private schools and boarding schools had a level of competency and control over their writing that I lacked. It was evident after the very first paper came back that I had a serious problem. Underneath the D the professor wrote, "You've clearly done a lot of research and read a lot, but this paper is poorly written." But he also offered this advice: "There's a writing center. You can go there and they'll teach you how to write."*
>
> *They opened at 7:30 in the morning. I went and said, "What's the limit? How many times a week can you come?" There was no limit, they said. I was floored. "You mean I could sign up for six hours a day, even on weekends?" They were like, "Yup." I said, "OK, I'd like the next three weeks, six hours a day."*
>
> *They were open at night. I wound up going all four years. I must have supported forty English graduate students single-handedly. I'd write my papers and come in for help. They were always surprised. They'd say, "When is this due?" and expect me to say, "This afternoon" or "Tomorrow." I'd say, "Six weeks from now." "And you're coming now?" they'd say, and I'd explain to them, "I know it's going to take me a lot of drafts, and I want to make sure I have time." I was writing very complex papers. I did original research on the CIA's takeover of Iran in 1954 and another paper on student communism in the 1930s, which involved extensive primary research. I must have gone through a hundred drafts on that one. It did not come easy. It was an uphill battle. But I worked incredibly hard on it and came out the other end knowing how to write.*

As many of our teachers and principals will attest, writing is the most difficult subject to teach—harder than reading, harder than math, harder than science and the rest—but we throw ourselves into it with passion and huge amounts of preparation, planning, and hard work. The results can be breathtaking. The process of making significant student progress and closing the achievement gap in this area can be slow and at times frustrating. A young student may write, "My face lit up like a firefly" one day and revert to "I was bored" the next. But we keep at it, and an essential step in the formula is that the scholars spend so much time in class writing and seeing their teachers model excellent writing for them.

"Part of the model is definitely more time on task. A big part of THINK Literacy is just giving kids ample time to read and write every day," said Michele Caracappa, principal of Success Academy Bronx 1. "That's the thing that makes our program very different from a lot of other schools, just providing those uninterrupted blocks of time when kids are reading and writing. We do believe deeply in building their stamina." The teachers' direct instruction at the start of each writing class lasts no more than ten minutes, but it exposes the students to a whole repertoire of best practices that excellent writers use and rely on.

Candido Brown, a dynamic first-grade teacher at Success Academy Harlem 2, now a fourth-grade teacher, gave a motivational speech that got his students fired up for writing at the first writing workshop. He explained to his kids beforehand that his aim was to "set the tone for a phenomenal year of writing. The biggest thing I want my kids to take away is that writing elevates them. It not only elevates their speech, it elevates their thinking and allows them to go higher and higher in college."

"Why do we write?" he asked the twenty-eight first graders, part of the college graduating class of 2026. "We write so that we put our ideas into the world. We want to make sure that people actually get a chance to hear and read about our thoughts, just like the authors of the books we read. This is the first thing we need to understand."

"Second—and this is important—writing elevates us. The more we write, the better speakers we become. Not only that, it elevates our thoughts, and it prepares us for college. Go ahead and close your eyes," he added. "Imagine that you've just walked into the world's most beautiful library. What are you seeing? You're seeing people sitting down, they're reading. What do you hear? No one is chatting, no one is eating in the library. Everyone is working. It's a calm place. It's tranquil. Just like that library I want our writers workshop to be a sacred place."

He told the young scholars, "Today we will write for seven minutes, but by the end of the year when you guys are getting ready for second grade, you won't write for thirty minutes, you won't write for thirty-one minutes. By the end of the year you will be able to write for forty minutes." Children's mouths fell open. "That's a lot of time you guys will have invested into writing. Writers become great writers by doing one important thing: writing. The more we write, the better we will become at writing."

This message is especially urgent for children who grow up in poverty. Mr. Brown said afterward that he personally felt a sense of urgency about teaching kids to write because "I know what it did for my life." He spent part of his childhood in inner-city Baltimore and went on to earn degrees from Johns Hopkins University and Harvard University. "I want to give it my all. It's dear to my heart. I went to two of the greatest institutions in the world . . . [and] I believe all of my children will get there as well."

That exemplifies the passion we bring to teaching writing. We'll look in this chapter at more examples of great writing instruction, but we'll also explore how hard we work to help teachers overcome the difficulties they face in helping turn their students into great, prolific, and insightful writers.

Setting Up Quality Independent Writing in First Grade   Clip 20

As you watch Mr. Brown set the tone for writing workshop in his first-grade class at the beginning of the year, you will no doubt be struck by his passion and enthusiasm for putting words on the page. *How could one not want to be a writer in his classroom?* We believe deeply that **kids get better at writing by writing,** but of course this only works if independent writing time is of high quality. In this video Mr. Brown sets the expectations and stage for high-level writing in his classroom. There are three parts to this critical writing workshop launch:

1. *The motivational speech.* As teachers of writing, we must *inspire* our scholars to write. We must make them want to be great writers.

2. *The setup routine.* In writing workshop it's critical that all materials are set up prior to direct instruction. This allows scholars to leave the meeting area after the lesson with a sense of urgency and purpose, with the day's teaching point top of mind. Establishing a setup routine from the get-go ensures that no negotiation of pens, paper, writing folders, or notebooks stands in the way of the teaching point's transferring into independent writing.

3. *Working the room.* During the early days of writing workshop, teachers must "work the room," **noticing 100 percent** of scholar behavior, correcting, and motivating as needed. This will set scholars up to practice constructive behaviors for the rest of the year.

Achieving writing excellence isn't easy, as every educator, every parent, and every child knows. In the age of instant messages and 140-character tweets, some may be deluded into thinking writing isn't as important as it once was. That's not where we want our scholars to be. The students who get into the best colleges, and who graduate into the best jobs and career opportunities, will always be the ones who can think critically and then put their ideas down on paper with both elegance and force—the ones who make readers hungry for more.

"Writing is an area we're still working on, but we set our bar really high and expect our kids to meet it," said Carrie Roby, principal of Success Academy Upper West. "We're always looking at student work, getting as many writing samples from other schools as we can to say, 'Well, what does really great writing look like?'" Even in our kindergarten and first-grade classes, teachers are looking for children's writing to convey a central idea. We spend weeks with our scholars in kindergarten through second grade on writing small-moment stories, encouraging them to capture the most interesting part of something that happened in their lives, whether it was a trip to the park or a visit to Grandma's house.

A precocious, talented second grader at Success Academy Harlem 3 turned the usual grandmother story on its head with an eight-page, six-hundred-word mystery she wrote over several weeks about an outing to a show at which someone steals the music and her brother is put in handcuffs for the crime. The real culprit is her evil grandmother.

> *"I can't wait to see the rehearsal!" Melanie shouted. "Calm down, it's still a few minutes until the rehearsal," Melanie's older sister noted.*
> *But the Music Palooza show couldn't go on without the sheet music.*
> *"Let's solve a mystery," Kevin yelled. "They will never solve this case," Grandma thought. Then she put an evil grin on her face.*

Eventually justice prevails. In an author's note, the second grader writes that her book "is about somebody who stole the Mozart score. Then it all leads to one person. Can you solve the mystery? Hope you enjoy."

Most seven- and eight-year-olds aren't writing stories replete with so much dialogue and that many twists and turns. But our teachers work tirelessly with the scholars to help them find the central idea of their writing. Often this happens in the small practice groups in which the teacher coaches six or more students at a time while the rest of the scholars are writing. It's important to let the students do the hard-thinking work. In regard to coaching students, we advise teachers not to do the intellectual heavy lifting *for* scholars ("Oh! So is the idea you're trying to show that . . . ?"). Instead we ask them, just like during read alouds, to ask great questions that lead to the eureka moment ("What do you want your readers to know when they read your story? What big idea do you want to leave your audience with?").

A WRITING LESSON FROM THE ICE RINK

The writing practice group in Kristina Kyle's kindergarten class at Success Academy Harlem 4 provides another good illustration of how we build on children's experiences in and out of school to sharpen their writing skills. When they start writing small-moment stories in kindergarten, "the whole day seems important," said Ms. Kyle. "We want them to zoom in on one specific part."

In the classroom Ms. Kyle told the six kindergartners in the small group, "I've pulled you together today because I've noticed you're writing wonderful stories with a really clear beginning, middle, and end, but we're going to practice something today that's going to make you an even better writer. We're going to practice zooming in on the part you really want to tell [so that readers can] experience it with us and make mind movies of exactly what we say in our stories." She recalled how the author Marla Frazee does that in one of their favorite books, *Roller Coaster*. (Later, Ms. Kyle noted that she was sending the scholars the message that "even though they are five and in kindergarten, they can be authors and do exactly what Marla Frazee does.")

She reminded them of the class outing to an ice skating rink, which was "a really special day for us. Do we want to tell when we got our skates and when we put them on and when we got on the ice and when we fell down and when we got hot chocolate and when we went home? Do we want to tell all that?"

"Noooo," the scholars said.

"No. We need to—"

"Zoom in."

"—Zoom in on the most important and the most meaningful part. Let's zoom in and tell it bit by bit and write it down in so much detail that our readers feel they're right there with us," Ms. Kyle told them.

She told them, "Close your eyes and imagine yourself right there by the ice, right before we took our steps. Tell me, what was your body doing, Chloe?"

"Shaking."

"Our knees were shaking," Ms. Kyle wrote down on the big sheet on her easel.

She asked them to remember walking out on the ice in one big group. What did that remind them of?

"It reminds me of a school of fish," a boy said.

She congratulated the students and told them that now it was their turn to zoom in on their own stories. She asked them to reread them "and think, What's the most important part I want to tell?"

Afterward Ms. Kyle remarked, "It's really easy for the teacher to say, 'Oh, this is the most important part of your story. Write about this.' But we want to be reflective and thoughtful about their writing and . . . coach them through with the right questions to find the most important part themselves. Questions like 'How are you feeling?' and 'What do you want your readers to know about this?' are going to help them find the deep meaning of their story."

A LESSON ON SWIMMING AND ON WRITING

At Success Academy Bronx 1 the personal story that kindergarten teacher Zoe Fonseca wrote and illustrated for her scholars during writing workshop was a perfect example of how to model rigorous, interesting, and well-crafted writing.

"Two days ago we were talking about getting ideas for small-moment stories," Ms. Fonseca told her twenty-six scholars. "One way to do this is to think of something you did that others would be interested in hearing about," she said. "Scholars, do you think others care about how I brushed my teeth?" Ms. Fonseca asked. The scholars gave a resounding no. "Maybe, however, you would want to know about that time when I was a little girl and I went to visit my relatives in Texas? I agree that sounds interesting."

"Let me zoom in. Grandpa taught me how to swim that summer, and at the end I surprised my Mom," she recalled, starting to draw pictures and write the words across three pages sitting on her Elmo projector. The first page showed her standing at the end of the diving board. On the second page she was swimming underwater across the pool. On the third page "my Mom is pulling me up out of the pool, getting herself all wet, she is so proud of me." Ms. Fonseca added the words to each story panel. *Midway I heard my mother scream, "You can do it."* Then, as she got out of the pool, *"I am so proud of you.*" The story ended this way: *I winked at my grandfather. He was a great teacher.*

Ms. Fonseca instructed the scholars to turn to their partner "and zoom in on one small thing" in the stories they were writing. She and Arin, who was observing this lesson, both got down on their knees to listen in as the students traded ideas and suggestions. The students started by drawing pictures on their three pages. "I'm going to show you how to write a sentence. Say it to yourself two times, then write it down," Ms. Fonseca told one pair.

A boy named Harel said he wanted to tell about the time his grandmother took him to the park. "Zoom in more, zoom in closer," his partner Jaylin coached him.

"I want to tell the part when my grandmother helped me go on the big kids' swing and helped me swing really high," said Harel.

"Now *that's* an important small moment," said Jaylin.

Michele Caracappa spoke with her teachers at Success Academy Bronx 1 about upping the rigor of their model writing after a Leader Study Group on this topic. "The wheels are starting to click on what a rigorous example is supposed to be, especially for the new teachers," she said. "We had a discussion about what rigorous writing instruction looked like. I had them video themselves and then watch each other's videos."

"Zoe wasn't writing pieces like that before. She thought it didn't make sense to share something like that with kindergartners, that it was too much for them," the principal said. Now she sees the merits of setting "an example beyond what they can do, because you want to inspire them about being excited about writing," even if they are still too young now to produce a story that good. "They're not going to pick up on it all in one day."

The Quality of Model Writing Matters Clip 21

So often teachers make the mistake of modeling writing in front of scholars that mirrors exactly what they can already do; that is, we model kindergarten-level writing for kindergartners. The problem with this, of course, is that the teacher's model writing sets the bar that kids will try to reach. So why would we set the bar at what they can do already? In these two segments Jackie Albers, principal of Success Academy Harlem 1, models the difference between low- and high-level writing, and demonstrates how **aiming high** will lift the level of rigor, excitement, and student writing, beginning in kindergarten.

THREE KEY COMPONENTS OF WRITING INSTRUCTION

THINK Literacy writing instruction includes writing workshop, shared writing, and interactive writing. Here's a primer on each.

1. *Writing workshop*. Scholars have a fifty- to sixty-minute writing workshop every day that provides long, uninterrupted stretches for writing. The purpose is for them to write voluminously with elegance and precision. The writing workshop teaches scholars to write in a variety of genres, crafting pieces with excellent ideas, structure, details, and mechanics. During the writing workshop the teacher gathers the class together and delivers a brief lesson—no longer than ten minutes—during which he or she models, and scholars get a brief opportunity to practice one aspect of excellent writing before the teacher sends the students back to their seats to write independently for an extended period. The time allocated for writing may start at seven minutes, as it did in Candido Brown's first-grade class, and grow steadily to as much as forty-five minutes. During this time the teacher pulls groups of six or more scholars together, as Kristina Kyle did, in writing practice groups, based on common weaknesses and strengths. Practice groups last ten to fifteen minutes, so the teacher works with multiple such groups during the writing block. Toward the end the teacher often allots five minutes for writing partnerships, having scholars pair off to critique each other's writing, and then he or she will wrap up the lesson by studying examples of excellent student work with scholars. Often that onetime, one-on-one coaching is all a student needs to get the point and catch up with the class. "The way we set up the writing workshop time allows teachers to meet the needs of all their kids," said Paola Zalkind, a founding kindergarten and then third-grade grade teacher, and now a Success Academy Harlem 2 leadership resident.

2. *Shared writing*. Scholars compose a piece of writing together, with the teacher acting as coach and scribe. The emphasis is on ideas, structure, and detail. Writing with the teacher helps the scholars internalize what it feels

and looks like to craft great writing. As with the teacher's model writing, the quality of the shared writing should be at a phenomenally high level to show the scholars what they are shooting for. Shared writing lasts ten to fifteen minutes and takes place two to three times each week.

3. *Interactive writing*. Interactive writing is used primarily in kindergarten through second grade. The emphasis is on writing mechanics. During interactive writing the teacher and scholars share the pen and write a piece, or a section of a piece, together. The scholars also practice writing words and phrases on individual whiteboards that the teacher can check at a glance. Interactive writing lasts fifteen minutes; it takes place four to five times each week in kindergarten and first grade, and as needed in higher grades.

Our curriculum and classes are aligned across the network, so it's possible for the principals, the leadership residents, and Eva and Arin to see the same writing lesson being taught by teachers in different classrooms at the same time.

The scholars are asked to do so much writing that sometimes it can be challenging for them to come up with new ideas. Teachers, too, can feel hard-pressed to keep coming up with cogent examples from their own lives for model writing. They may look in vain for moments of high drama or comic relief. But here our advice to children and adults alike is to just be real and honest and write about what's on our mind. It doesn't have to be about the time we burned the cookies at Christmas or took our first roller coaster ride or lost the dog. The most compelling stories come from the things about which we care deeply. It's this investment that makes the story, not the uproarious ending or the O. Henry twist.

Vanessa Bangser, principal of Success Academy Bronx 2, tells her teachers to draw on the same skills they use to tell a funny story to friends after work. "The skills you use to tell hilarious stories to friends at the end of the day shouldn't be different from the skills you're modeling in your writing piece in the classroom," she said. Vanessa also advises her teachers not to "overthink it or force it, but have it be more natural." Instead of trying to cram a thousand strategies into the lesson, "highlight one particular thing, like having great details or a lot of dialogue or being humorous, and just focusing on that instead of drawing attention to every single thing you do."

Teachers are "going to model enough pieces throughout the unit to highlight all the things they want," the principal said. "Every piece of good writing will have many good qualities, but you don't need to stop and draw attention to every one."

In one of Success Academy Bronx 2's first-grade classrooms, teacher Jodie Brenner was following Vanessa's advice. "Think of a topic that matters to you, someone or something you love, something you love doing, a place that's important to you. Think, think, think. When you have it, hold it up in the air," she said. "Now, think deeper. What is the big idea you want to show? Not just that you love your mom or the park. Why? Why do you love these things so much? What do they do for you?"

In most first-grade classrooms teachers are happy when students are writing simple sentences. In Success Academies, however, we want the scholars to show a central idea to their writing. They may still be writing about the commonplace themes of six- and seven-year-olds' lives—birthday parties, toys, presents, pets—but already they are trying to drill deeper. For the first go-round they could pick topics like "My shiny red bike is the best present I've ever gotten" or "My little brother is so annoying." And they are going to have many more bites of this apple.

Clip 22   Writing Direct Instruction, Second Grade

As you watch Dionne Beckford, then a second-grade teacher at Success Academy Harlem 1, teach her second-grade scholars to write their stories with bit-by-bit action at pivotal parts, notice the following **evidence of high-level intellectual preparation:**

- Ms. Beckford understands her teaching point inside and out, so she's able to convey its purpose and utility to scholars.

- Ms. Beckford has crafted her own model writing at a high level. She knows *exactly* what she is going to write in front of scholars, and therefore she is able to model the teaching point effectively.

- Even though this is not today's teaching point, **Ms. Beckford has crafted a model story with a strong central idea.** We stress the importance of central ideas in writing beginning in kindergarten, so our teachers must always practice what they preach when it comes to their model writing. Ms. Beckford's story shows how the energy of the crowd as she ran through Harlem revitalized her during the New York City Marathon.

- Ms. Beckford has studied her kids' writing in order to set them up to practice the teaching point briefly but authentically during the lesson.

WRITING ACROSS THE CURRICULUM

We teach the craft of writing in almost every subject, including chess. Sean O'Hanlon, the chess teacher at Success Academy Harlem 2, majored in American literature in college and earned a master's degree in poetry. "I try to get the kids writing as much as I can," he said. He had just wheeled out of a third-grade classroom a cart of Mac laptops on which the students play chess. Their writing assignment that afternoon had been to analyze three diagrams of chess positions. The best looked like the explanatory text in a newspaper chess column. "They had to write an explanation of each one. They wrote everything," Sean said. "That's on the third-grade level. In kindergarten it's simple things like getting kids to write the name of the piece and words like *capture* and *protect*." But his third graders "had to describe each position and then try to put all those positions together to come up with what's the main idea: What's going on in each of these positions? What do they have in common? Then they had to come up with their own title," he explained.

Dealing with tricky word problems in math and learning how to write scientific hypotheses also hone our students' writing skills and precision. One reason we take our scholars to so many interesting places—on field trips to the circus, to farms, to museums, to college campuses—is so they will have an enriched band of experiences to enjoy and to write about. "Writing is our biggest need," said Paola Zalkind. "If you look at the difference between our kids' writing and [that of] the kids at affluent private schools, we still have much catching up to do. In writing, the achievement gap is the widest so we have to work really hard at it, but we are gaining ground and fast."

Success Academy Harlem 2 principal Jim Manly said that teaching writing is harder than teaching reading or math. "It's the most laborious and time intensive," he said. "Your first temptation is just to do it for them, to give them the sentence: 'Well, what you're trying to say is . . .' To really work with the kids and have them learn how to start to organize thoughts and put them down in sentences and help them grow is an intense process."

Jim Manly, Paola Zalkind, Carrie Roby, and other leaders spent an entire morning in a Leader Study Group working on upping the rigor of their teachers' writing lessons. They viewed videotapes of teachers before and after coaching, practiced on each other, and then went into classrooms and taught writing lessons to children while colleagues watched and critiqued them. And, back at their respective schools, they spread the gospel to classroom teachers about the importance of serving as writing role models for their students.

JAZZING UP THE WRITING

Our teachers work hard to show the scholars how to make their writing more interesting.

One morning teachers Lela Rosen and Kate Hazleton at Success Academy Harlem 2 were showing two dozen second graders how to jazz up the "expert" book each was writing on a topic he or she knew a lot about. "We've been working really hard on our 'All About . . .' topic books, and you've been adding so many wonderful details and facts under each chapter heading," said Ms. Rosen. "But we've been noticing your information is a little dry. We want to spice up that writing, just like we do for our fiction stories."

"So today we're going to teach you that writers help our readers understand our topic better by comparing it to something else," said Ms. Hazleton.

"I have a book to share with you, and it's called *The Life Cycle of a Cat*. I picked up this book because I have a cat named Annie at home and I thought it might be interesting to read," said Ms. Hazleton, projecting the book on the classroom's Elmo. She read: "A cat begins life as a kitten. Kittens are small when they are born. Their eyes are closed. They cannot hear . . ."

"Ahhh," said some scholars.

"The mother cat takes care of kittens. She carries them with her mouth."

"Eeeew," scholars chorused to express their distaste for this method of conveyance. The teacher resumed her recitation: "Kittens grow quickly. They can see and hear after ten days."

"You know, Ms. Hazleton, I'm finding this information interesting; obviously we all had a reaction to some of the facts. But honestly, the writing is kind of boring. It's not interesting. It's not really jazzed up," said Ms. Rosen. "I have this book over here that might help us." She handed it to her teaching partner.

"I'm going to read you one quick page I noticed that really stood out to me: 'In a small quake, dishes rattle, ceiling lights swing, the ground jiggles a bit as if a big truck were going by. It's all over in a few seconds,'" read Ms. Hazleton.

"You know what I love right there? 'The ground jiggles a bit as if a big truck were going by,'" repeated Ms. Rosen. Do you see how this writer compares the topic to something else? It's so much more interesting. It's almost like show and not tell, but for nonfiction writing."

> "I've never been in an earthquake before, but I can almost imagine how it feels," said Ms. Hazleton. "I know what it feels like when a truck goes by." They set to work modeling for the class how to jazz up the introduction to an expert book that Ms. Rosen had written and showed the class earlier.

PRACTICE MAKES PERFECT

In another second-grade class also working on nonfiction writing, teacher Amy Althoff at Success Academy Harlem 2 pulled six scholars together for a writing practice group on how to make their writing more interesting. She showed them a page she had written about one of her favorite activities, gardening, as an example of what not to do. She turned to the section on composting.

> "Every sentence starts with the same word: 'Compost is so cool. Compost is in the garden. Compost is in a bin.' Compost, compost, compost. How does your reader feel about that?" Ms. Althoff asked.
>
> "Bor-ing," the scholars replied in unison.
>
> "It is kind of boring when you start everything with the same word," said the teacher as she began quickly rewriting the beginnings of each sentence, varying each opening. "Did you see how I made my writing interesting by changing up the way I start my sentences? It makes it really cool for my readers. I want you guys to get your paper out and think about the way you can change the beginning of your sentences so your reader is really excited to look at them. I'm going to come around and watch you. If you've got a really good one, just put your quiet thumb up so you can share it with the group," said Ms. Althoff.

Outside, Arin called this one of the best writing practice groups she had seen. Ms. Althoff took the lesson on sentence structure and "made it totally clear and interesting to the scholars. She linked conventions to ideas. The kids understood why they were there. It was down and dirty. It took only two minutes and they were writing."

Things weren't going anywhere near that well in another second-grade class, in which the students were working on books they were writing about their favorite pastime, from football to chess to video games. A boy enamored of his Xbox wrote, "You just push the button to turn the Xbox on."

That wasn't the explanation his teacher was looking for. "But I don't know how to play Xbox. I've never done it. What can you teach me?" she asked. Mr. Manly, trying to help, interjected, "Do you have a silly cousin? How would you help them learn to play if they came over?" To the others, he added, "This is true for all your pieces." Afterward, in a postmortem with other leaders, the principal said these students might have come closer to the mark if the teacher had done a better job of modeling what a how-to book should look like.

The writing instruction was on a much higher level in the third-grade class of Courtney Olsen. Ms. Olsen, who is now a leadership resident at Success Academy Harlem 4, had just modeled how to write about everyday things she observed in the classroom. At their desks the scholars filled two columns headed "What I See" and "This Makes Me Think . . ." One boy looked at the classroom door and wrote, "You have to be careful because you can get your fingers caught in the door."

Ms. Olsen called four scholars to a horseshoe-shaped desk and said, "Remember, when we observe we look carefully, we describe, and we think with our senses. And then we just start writing. And as I started writing I came up with even more ideas, and all of a sudden it *blossomed* into something that seemed like a real writer wrote it. That's what I want you to do."

Ms. Olsen continued, "I see Anthony has started with the beach. I want you to choose anything in our room and the world around us. Anything you want to describe. Observe it in your mind, and then start writing." She pirouetted around the horseshoe, probing scholars on their ideas and getting them to expand on them without suggesting other topics or how to make them more interesting. Quickly she dispatched all but one struggling student back to their desks, leaving her more time to work one-on-one with him.

We were there with Mr. Manly to observe this lesson and gave it glowing reviews. "She was pushing, pushing, pushing the kids to think deeper, whereas 90 percent of the teachers would have said, 'So you think this?' and given them an idea," said Arin. "She really helped the kids see what they wanted to write about, what their idea was, and she let them struggle a bit. She didn't jump in to save them. She showed she believed they could have an idea and a better one and an even better one. That's rare."

"She finished with the kids who got it instead of getting lost in the one who was really struggling, and then got back to help him," said Mr. Manly.

"I loved her high-level example of how you select an object and write meaningful and elegant things about it," said Eva. "That's one of the hallmarks of rigor. Also, she kept saying, 'I want to know what you think.' Kids tend to parrot back what the teacher says. Courtney was very disciplined." But she added that if the purpose of the lesson had been to enhance students' powers of observation, it might have been better to ask them to look at a painting and make observations about that rather than having some eyeing the classroom door. It is hard for eight- and nine-year-olds to make good choices about what to observe.

A POWERFUL ENDING TO A PERSONAL NARRATIVE

Writing Direct Instruction, Fourth Grade Clip 23

Andrea Klein, formerly a fourth-grade teacher at Success Academy Harlem 1 and now part of the network literacy team, offered a great example of model writing. It was a true story that she wrote about a visit to see her dying grandmother.

Mrs. Klein showed her students how her personal narrative, titled "Realization," went through different drafts. For the first draft she wrote:

Across the table I saw Mammy lying on the duvet. Her toes showed from under the blanket that covered her.

"Andrea, what are you reading?" Mammy asked.

"One of your favorites," I replied. "Angle of Repose by Stegner."

Mammy looked at me. "I love that novel. It's one of my favorites." With her eyes closed, she whispered, "I sure do love you beautiful girl; I am so blessed." I felt as if I was going to cry but tried hard not to. "I love you, too," I said.

I tried to read to distract myself from being so sad. Mammy wasn't just resting. She was very sick. Soon I knew I would be back at my grandparents' house seeing visitors as they stopped by to give their condolences. I already missed her.

Mrs. Klein told the class, "Now I'm going to write the ending. I'm going to write a strong image ending, and then I am going to make revisions." With the projector showing the class her work, Mrs. Klein began her revisions.

The sun beat through the clear glass windows of my parents' sun porch. Across the glass coffee table, I saw Mammy, reclined on the floral, overstuffed duvet, her delicate painted toes poking out from under the afghan that covered her.

"Andrea, what book are you reading?" Mammy inquired in a voice so soft I barely heard her.

"One of your favorites, actually," I replied. " Angle of Repose by Stegner."

Mammy lifted her head slightly and turned her sparkling blue eyes toward me. "I love that novel—the heartbreak of the main characters, the unbridled wild of the West. All of it just sings to me. The setting is simply serene. Heavenly." She took a shallow breath and placed her curly head back on the pillow. With her eyes closed, she whispered, "I sure do love you beautiful girl; I am so blessed."

I gulped back the tears and sob that formed in the back of my throat. "I love you, too," I managed to whisper. I tried to read to distract myself from the deep sorrow that filled my body. Mammy wasn't just resting. Her body was giving out on her. Soon, I knew, I would be back at my grandparents' house. It would be transformed into a busy hive of activity with cousins, aunts and uncles seeing visitors as they stopped by to give condolences. I already missed her.

Mrs. Klein looked at the class and said, "So, scholars, now that I have this great small moment, I want to go on and add a powerful ending. I think the strongest way to convey my main idea is . . . to describe that moment. I'll simply start with 'I watched.'" She continued, "I watched as Mammy fell into a deep slumber." ("Here I'm going to repeat the image of the sunlight coming through," she told the class.) "Streaks of soft sunlight illuminated—kind of lit up, illuminated—her beautifully aged cheek. In that moment I could see the West Texas beauty queen she had once been."

It was a powerful ending, and a powerful lesson in writing that pulls readers in and touches their heart.

TAKEAWAYS

PRINCIPALS: Don't be lulled into neglecting writing by the presence of all those multiple-choice questions on state English language arts tests. World-class schools must make writing a top priority. Every member of the school community must place a high value on writing clearly, elegantly, and concisely. Writing is your moral obligation as school leaders. It will get your children into selective colleges, and it is a lifelong skill that your students need. Excellent writing is achieved through practice. School leaders—lead on the writing front.

TEACHERS: Inspire your students, even the kindergartners, with your passion for writing. If your students are to write at a high level, so, too, must you. Practice your model writing. Seek help. If you're rusty or lack confidence, take a writing course. Read excellent writing. Do not run out of time for writing. Study your students' writing constantly. This is how you will know where to go next, and whether your teaching is sticking! Celebrate your students' writing by reading it aloud daily and with publishing celebrations. Turn your students into authors and change their life trajectories by doing so.

PARENTS: Demand that your child's public school have a strong emphasis on writing and that teachers get the training they need to be great writing instructors. The entire school community must be passionate about the importance of writing. This can't wait until third grade or fifth grade. Great writing starts in kindergarten and first grade. If you don't see it, demand to know why.

SCHOOL REFORMERS: As you embrace national policies to fundamentally reform schools, do not forget about writing. Writing is a powerful lever for learning. We need to teach it. We (adults and children) need to practice it. We need to insist on rigorous writing standards and hold schools accountable for meeting them. It's much more labor intensive than giving multiple-choice tests, but children will be held back in life if they cannot write exceptionally well.

CHAPTER EIGHT

CALL TO ACTION

How to Make Every School a Success Academy

Our call to action is directed to parents, teachers, principals, policymakers, tax-payers, and concerned citizens.

Our nation's schools are a mess.

It's not just urban schools or minority kids. The picture is the same in city after city, suburb after suburb, rural community after rural community. The schools aren't aiming high enough. They're far too easy. The yardsticks states use to measure student performance are a joke. Success Academies have bolted to the top of the rankings in New York City and New York State, and we're acutely aware that's not good enough.

New York has made its grading scale a little tougher, but it still comes up with a lot more high-scoring students than the much tougher National Assessment of Educational Progress (NAEP).

NAEP tells us that one-third of all four million fourth graders in the United States cannot read at a basic level. One-third! And American kids, compared to their counterparts around the world, fall further behind as they get to senior year of high school—if they get to senior year of high school.

As President Barack Obama has said, "The status quo is unacceptable." He summarized the situation in a recent speech at a Boston high school: "Today, as many as a quarter of American students are not finishing high school—a quarter. The quality of our math and science education lags behind many other nations. And America has fallen to ninth in the proportion of young people with a college degree. We used to be number one, and we're now number nine. That's not acceptable."[1]

Massachusetts happens to be the state with the toughest standards and the highest scores on national exams like NAEP. The average student in Massachusetts winds up as much as four grade levels above the average kid in the worst states in reading and math, according to the American Institutes for Research.[2] But even Massachusetts kids are outscored by kids in more than a dozen countries.[3]

It's not just Singapore, South Korea, and Japan that are putting our schools to shame. It's Finland and Canada. A dozen of the world's most prosperous countries now graduate more students from college, and only eight of the thirty-four countries in the Organisation for Economic Co-operation and Development (OECD) have worse high school dropout rates.[4]

On the OECD's Programme for International Student Assessment, a test given to half a million fifteen-year-olds around the world, about one in ten American youth reached the next-to-the-top achievement level in math. Twice that many scored that high in South Korea, Switzerland, Finland, and Belgium; three times that many in Singapore and Hong Kong; and five times that many in Shanghai, China. In science, 1 percent of American kids scored at the top level, compared to nearly 4 percent in New Zealand and nearly 5 percent in Singapore.[5]

In California, one kid in thirty drops out *before* he or she gets to high school.[6]

Starting in Harlem and the Bronx, we're trying to rewrite this script. As we showed you earlier in this book, our kindergartners are taught science and do experiments every day. Our scholars spend up to three hours a day in THINK Literacy classes that are making them voracious readers and prolific writers.

We're setting them on the path that leads straight to college graduation and the doors that open up beyond that to becoming scientists, doctors, lawyers, teachers, and members of other professions that are vital to our country's future.

People wonder how we do it. Our secret sauce is no secret.

Our schools are full of joyful rigor. We've set the standards high for the children and the adults. We give them the time, the training, and the support they need to do what most people thought impossible in schools in which most students are black or brown and living in poverty or just above it.

We're getting these phenomenal results with kids who have been selected at random by lottery, not those pretested for admission to highly selective schools. Yet our students are performing as well as the children in those "gifted and talented" programs.

We've written this book to show others what we're doing and encourage them to try our methods.

The most important advice we can give you is to start with the adults. They hold the key to high achievement. It's the adults, not the children, who need to step up their game.

We're a network of public charter schools, so we aren't bound by some of the hindrances that other public schools face. We've got more freedom to choose whom we hire and whom we let go. We teach and work longer hours (and also earn higher pay), and our principals, their assistants, and the teachers get more time to train, prepare, and practice lessons and develop their professional skills than in schools anywhere else we know.

It may be tempting for other educators to use those differences as an excuse; to say, "Oh, they can do it because they don't have to deal with all the kids who need special education or who are still learning English or who are poor." That's wrong. We have just as many of those kids as the schools around us. They may say, "Success Academies don't have to deal with the unions." That's true, but other schools don't have to go through the struggles we've faced to move into underused space in neighborhood schools and to do it with thousands of dollars less in city and state funding for our pupils.

Let's leave the bitterly contested politics of school funding and school reform aside for now. Charter schools are here to stay. They've sprung up across the country in the past decade because so many regular public schools were not getting the job done. Some charter schools are no better than those other schools. But ours are great. And we think our approach and methods—embracing rigor, working intensively with the grown-ups to improve their teaching skills, and demanding excellence from all—can work in schools everywhere, public or charter.

It's time for all of us—teachers, parents, policymakers, and the public at large—to demand action and to take decisive steps. America's public schools are in desperate shape, worse than even their harshest critics realize. The country's future is riding on our ability to turn them around. The record of Success Academies shows this can be done.

We think the solutions most commonly offered to fix public schools are barking up the wrong tree. We've been obsessed with the wrong things, like class size, merit pay, and school funding. We spend more than any country in the world on K–12 education, and what do we have to show for it? Mediocrity or worse.

Our laser-like focus instead should be on the things that really make a difference in schools, such as the quality of books; the rigor and breadth of the curriculum; the amount of training for the teachers; and whether the principal has the time, freedom, and skills to be the school's instructional leader.

Lawmakers and school leaders are consumed with how to hold classroom teachers more accountable for student performance. We're certainly not against accountability. But it doesn't solve the problem. Strict accountability measures help you make the diagnosis, but we need to focus on the efficacy of the instruction to address the root causes of school failure. If teachers learn how to teach more effectively, student achievement can and will go up.

School reformers often pay lip service to the importance of the principal but don't then advocate for policies that would dramatically improve the leadership at the school level. It's a huge undertaking in a country with fourteen thousand school districts and nearly a hundred thousand schools. But it's crucial. Teachers cannot get better if the principal doesn't constantly improve as well. We need principals who can step up to the plate and truly be the instructional leaders and inspirations for their school. Instead of expending huge amounts of time and energy on rooting out the bottom dwellers, we need to concentrate on getting the vast majority of teachers the on-the-job coaching, training, and mentoring they need to play at the top of their game. We don't need to wait for Superman to come along, and we're not asking for superhuman efforts by teachers. We've got to do this ourselves. Principals, teachers, and parents cannot wait for others and must take responsibility for making their schools much, much better.

The number of charter schools has been growing exponentially. They've introduced a healthy amount of competition to the much larger, regular public school system. But we need both charter and regular schools to get better to execute a real turnaround in American education. Great schools like ours provide a model for others to follow. We're an experiment, a clinical trial, and our results demonstrate what is possible if all schools were to pursue excellence with our passion and determination. We've shattered the myth that most poor and minority children are incapable of high achievement, and the myth that demography is destiny. Other countries with equal percentages of poor and immigrant children are teaching them much more than American schoolkids are learning. All children can learn, but they cannot reach their potential if the adults do not reach theirs.

The time is now. Our kids cannot wait. Parents, teachers, principals, policymakers, taxpayers, and concerned citizens: we need action. Here's what we must do:

1. *Understand that rigor is the innovation that will save American public education*. Embracing rigor is the most profound way to change schooling. This won't happen by magic. It takes lots and lots of hard work. But it's doable.

- *Remember it's all about the grown-ups, not the children.* The only sure way to give children a world-class education is to begin with the teachers and give them the professional development and coaching they need to dramatically improve their teaching ability.

- *Look to leaders first.* The education debate for years has focused on teachers and evaluation to the exclusion of almost everything else. We can't fix teaching without first fixing school leadership. Principals must act as instructional leaders, not building managers.

- *Partner with the parents.* We couldn't do what we're doing without 110 percent support from Success Academy parents. When they entrust their child to us, they agree to read all the time; closely monitor the homework; work with the teacher; and take part in a host of school activities, including Saturday classes if needed. Opponents of charters say this explains our success because our parents are far more engaged than the typical public school parent. But partnering is a two-way street. We keep our classroom doors open for parents to visit every day, and we keep the two-way lines of communication open. We call parents with good news about their child as well as about any problems. Partnership, like marriage, takes a lot of hard work, but it pays off.

- *Move teacher training from campuses to schools.* Schools of education have failed us, turning out graduates who are ill-prepared for the challenging job ahead of them. They've proven resistant to reform and demands for higher standards. Schools like ours already serve as the clinical training grounds for many novice teachers. The best schools should play a bigger role in training and credentialing new teachers.

- *Stop looking at reform through the wrong lenses.* The endless debates about class size, merit pay, and school funding miss the point. Focus instead on the real levers for change and high achievement, including the rigor of the curriculum, the quality of books, the leadership within the school, and the amount of training for teachers to enable them to grow on the job.

- *Stop obsessing over teacher accountability, and focus instead on efficacy.* We're all for accountability. Great teachers make a difference. But we should be more concerned about the efficacy of teaching and leading and what teachers need to be successful. It is not necessarily smaller classes or better evaluation tools. What they need is rigorous training and school leaders who have been trained to lead and manage at an exceptionally high level.

You don't have to be a Success Academy or even a charter school to do what we're doing: helping our teachers grow as professionals; doing things fast and wasting no time in helping children master lessons and move on to the next challenge; and offering a rich, imaginative curriculum that emphasizes reading, writing, and critical thinking skills without sacrificing science, the arts, sports, and other activities that lay the groundwork for college and successful careers.

Let's stop making excuses for mediocrity and failure. Great schools can make all the difference in children's lives, regardless of other challenges they face. The task for educators is not to find a cure for poverty (or bemoan the absence of a cure), but to become extraordinarily good at their job. Other countries do this. So can we.

We've endeavored in these pages and in the videotaped lessons that accompany this book to demonstrate what is possible when parents demand excellence and educators deliver it. Changing the trajectory of students' lives is hard work, but it's also tremendously uplifting, rewarding, and inspiring.

We're proud of Success Academies, but don't think we have a monopoly or exclusive franchise on great schooling. What matters at the end of the day is not the type or structure of the school your child attends, but whether all adults therein truly believe that every child can learn, whether they have strong leadership, and whether they are willing to undertake the hard work that makes world-class schooling possible.

So this is our call to action. Join us on this frontal assault against the achievement gap and against mediocrity in public education. To fellow educators we say forget what you think is "realistic" or possible and rethink just how much YOU are capable of and how fast and far your students can move with inspired teaching. To parents we say this cannot be done without you as our partners, not just checking the homework but also demanding more and pushing your school to prepare your child for college from the first day of kindergarten. To policymakers we say don't let rules and regulations or entrenched interests stand in the way of letting schools achieve excellence. We need more freedom and encouragement and less red tape. Don't be afraid of competition. It's what made America great and what may yet save American education. Already we see a new day dawning for public education. The future is in our hands.

ENDNOTES

CHAPTER 1

1. Editorial Projects in Education, *Diplomas Count 2011: Beyond High School, Before Baccalaureate—Meaningful Alternatives to a Four-Year Degree,* June 2011, www.edweek.org/ew/toc/2011/06/09/index.html. Available with subscription.

2. Children's Defense Fund, *The State of America's Children 2011,* July 18, 2011, www.childrensdefense.org/soac.

3. National Center for Education Statistics (NCES), *The Nation's Report Card: Reading 2011* (NCES 2012-457) (Washington DC: Institute of Education Sciences, U.S. Department of Education, November 2011), http://nces.ed.gov/nationsreportcard/pdf/main2011/2012457.pdf.

4. McKinsey & Company, *The Economic Impact of the Achievement Gap in America's Schools,* April 2009, www.partnersinschools.org/resources /McKinsey%20&%20Co.%20Report.pdf.

5. Organisation for Economic Co-operation and Development (OECD), *Strong Performers and Successful Reformers in Education: Lessons from PISA for the United States,* 2011, 15, www.oecd.org/dataoecd/32/50/46623978.pdf.

6. OECD, *Strong Performers,* 15.

7. OECD, *Strong Performers,* 28–29.

8. "Prepared Remarks by Bill Gates, Co-Chair and Trustee" (speech to the National Urban League, Boston, July 27, 2011), www.gatesfoundation.org /speeches-commentary/Pages/bill-gates-2011-urban-league.aspx.

9. McKinsey & Company, "Economic Impact," 7.

10. E. A. Hanushek, P. E. Peterson, and L. Woessmann, *U.S. Math Performance in Global Perspective: How Well Does Each State Do at Producing High-Achieving Students?* (PEPG Report no. 10–19),

November 2010, 4, www.hks.harvard.edu/pepg/PDF/Papers/PEPG10
-19_HanushekPetersonWoessmann.pdf.

11. Hanushek, Peterson, and Woessmann, *U.S. Math Performance*, 4.

12. Hanushek, Peterson, and Woessmann, *U.S. Math Performance*, 4.

13. J. P. Greene and J. B. McGee, "When the Best Is Mediocre," *Education
     Next* 12, no. 1 (Winter 2012), http://educationnext.org/when-the-best-is
     -mediocre/?utm_source=feedburner&utm_medium=email&utm_campaign
     =Feed:+EducationNext+%28Education+Next%29.

14. Greene and McGee, "When the Best Is Mediocre."

15. Barack Obama, "Remarks by the President on Education Reform at the
     National Urban League Centennial Conference" (speech to the National
     Urban League, Washington Convention Center, Washington DC, July 29,
     2010), www.whitehouse.gov/the-press-office/remarks-president-education
     -reform-national-urban-league-centennial-conference.

16. "Fast Facts," National Center for Education Statistics, accessed January 27,
     2012, http://nces.ed.gov/fastfacts/display.asp?id=372.

17. National Education Association Research, *Rankings of the States
     2010 and Estimates of School Statistics 2011,* December 2010,
     www.nea.org/assets/docs/HE/NEA_Rankings_and_Estimates010711.pdf.

18. J. Schmitt, K. Warner, and S. Gupta, *The High Budgetary Cost of Incarcera-
     tion* (Washington DC: Center for Economic and Policy Research, June 2010).
     The authors estimate average incarceration costs of $25,500 per federal pris-
     oner and $26,000 per state prisoner and per jail inmate.

19. National Center for Education Statistics, *Digest of Education Statistics*, Table
     64. "Public and private elementary and secondary teachers, enrollment, and
     pupil/teacher ratios: Selected years, fall 1955 through fall 2018." Down-
     loaded from http://nces.ed.gov/programs/digest/d09/tables/dt09_064.asp.

20. NCES, *Nation's Report Card: Reading 2011;* National Center for Edu-
     cation Statistics (NCES), *The Nation's Report Card: Mathematics
     2011* (NCES 2012-458) (Washington DC: Institute of Educa-
     tion Sciences, U.S. Department of Education, November 2011),
     http://nces.ed.gov/nationsreportcard/pdf/main2011/2012458.pdf.

21. Arne Duncan, "Lessons from High-Performing Countries" (speech at the National Center on Education and the Economy National Symposium, Washington DC, May 21, 2011), www.ed.gov/news/speeches/lessons-high -performing-countries.

22. NCES, *Nation's Report Card: Mathematics 2011*.

23. Organisation for Economic Co-operation and Development, *PISA 2009 Results: What Students Know and Can Do; Student Performance in Reading, Mathematics and Science,* vol. 1, 2010, www.oecd.org/dataoecd/10/61/48852548.pdf.

24. P. E. Peterson, L. Woessmann, E. A. Hanushek, and C. X. Lastra-Anadón, "Are U.S. Students Ready to Compete?" *Education Next* 11, no. 4 (Fall 2011), http://educationnext.org/are-u-s-students-ready-to-compete/.

25. National Center for Education Statistics, *Digest of Education Statistics*, Table 64. "Public and private elementary and secondary teachers, enrollment, and pupil/teacher ratios: Selected years, fall 1955 through fall 2018." Downloaded from http://nces.ed.gov/programs/digest/d09/tables/dt09_064.asp.

26. J. Coleman, T. Hoffer, and S. Kilgore. *Public and Private Schools* (report to the National Center for Education Statistics by the National Opinion Research Center, April 1981).

27. National Catholic Educational Association, "United States Catholic Elementary and Secondary Schools 2010–2011: The Annual Statistical Report on Schools, Enrollment and Staffing." Retrieved from http://www.ncea.org/news/annualdatareport.asp.

28. National Center for Education Statistics, "1.5 Million Homeschooled Students in the United States in 2007" (NCES 2009-030), *Issue Brief,* December 2008, http://nces.ed.gov/pubs2009/2009030.pdf.

29. "Facts," Center for Education Reform, accessed January 25, 2012, www.edreform.com/issues/choice-charter-schools/facts/.

30. J. Klein, "The Failure of American Schools," *Atlantic,* June 2011, 4, www.theatlantic.com/magazine/archive/2011/06/the-failure-of-american -schools/8497/.

31. Arne Duncan, speech at OECD's release of the Program for International Student Assessment (PISA) 2009 results, Dec. 7, 2010. Retrieved Feb. 23, 2011,

from http://www.ed.gov/news/speeches/secretary-arne-duncans-remarks
-oecds-release-program-international-student-assessment.

32. Eric Hanushek, "The Trade-off Between Child Quantity and Quality." *Journal of Political Economy*, 100(1), February 1992, pp. 84–117.

33. M. Gladwell, *What the Dog Saw and Other Adventures,* 318, Little, Brown and Company, New York, October, 2009.

CHAPTER TWO

1. "Prepared Remarks by Bill Gates, Co-Chair and Trustee" (speech to the National Urban League, Boston, July 27, 2011), www.gatesfoundation.org /speeches-commentary/Pages/bill-gates-2011-urban-league.aspx.

CHAPTER THREE

1. B. Auguste, P. Kihn, M., Miller, "Closing the Talent Gap: Attracting and Retaining Top-Third Graduates to Careers in Teaching," p. 5, McKinsey and Company, September 2010. Retrieved Feb. 23, 2012, from http://mckinseyonsociety.com/downloads/reports/Education/Closing_the _talent_gap.pdf.

CHAPTER FIVE

1. New York Times School Book "Q&A with Jackie Albers." No date given. Retrieved from http://www.nytimes.com/schoolbook/school/1616-harlem -success-academy-1-charter-school/principal.

2. S. Covey, A. Merrill, R. Merrill, *First Things First: To Live, to Love, to Learn, to Leave a Legacy*. New York: Simon and Schuster, 1994.

CHAPTER EIGHT

1. "President Obama on Education at TechBoston," (speech at TechBoston, Boston, March 8, 2011), www.whitehouse.gov/photos-and -video/video/2011/03/09/president-obama-education-techboston#transcript.

2. G. W. Phillips, *International Benchmarking: State Educational Performance Standards,* American Institutes for Research, October 2010, www.air.org/files/AIR_Int_Benchmarking_State_Ed Perf_Standards.pdf.

3. E. Hanushek, P. Peterson, and L. Woessmann, "Teaching Math to the Talented," *Education Next* 11, no. 1 (Winter 2011), http://educationnext.org/teaching-math-to-the-talented/.

4. Organization for Economic Cooperation and Development (OECD), "Lessons from PISA for the United States: Strong Performers and Successful Reformers in Education," OECD Publishing (2011), p. 15. http://www.oecd.org/dataoecd/32/50/46623978.pdf.

5. Organisation for Economic Co-operation and Development, *PISA 2009 Results: What Students Know and Can Do; Student Performance in Reading, Mathematics and Science,* vol. 1, 2010, www.oecd.org/dataoecd/10/61/48852548.pdf.

6. California Department of Education, *State Report (2008–09 Dropout Report),* accessed January 25, 2012, http://api.cde.ca.gov/Acnt2011/2010BaseStApi_drop.aspx?allcds=0000000.

ACKNOWLEDGMENTS

There are so many people who are a part of running our schools that it is hard to name them all, and we will surely forget a few.

We are grateful to Joel Greenblatt and John Petry, who had the vision to develop a replicable school model and have supported and guided us from the beginning. Our board chairs and network board members, Richard Pzena, Doug Hirsch, Lance Rosen, Gideon Stein, John Rowan, Steve Galbraith, Rich Barrera, Sam Martini, Dan Nir, Daniel Loeb, Yen Liow, David Greenspan, Rob Goldstein, and Jim Peyser, and our very generous funders, have helped ensure that our focus can remain on the children.

We're grateful to Paul Fucaloro, a cofounder of Success Academy Charter Schools who is the most talented educator we have ever met, and to Jenny Sedlis, a cofounder who battles the forces of the status quo with great skill and aplomb, allowing us to focus on instruction (and who was a key thought partner throughout the writing of this book).

We are indebted to our nine outstanding principals, who lead with urgency, commitment, and skill: Jackie Albers, Jim Manly, Richard Seigler, Danique Loving, Stacey Apatov, Michele Caracappa, Vanessa Bangser, Monica Burress, and Carrie Roby.

We're immensely grateful to the outstanding teachers in our schools who are committed to improving their craft and are relentless about achieving success for children. You are changing the world with your passion, talent, and dedication to excellence.

We're grateful to the fantastic families who are part of the Success Academy community. You trust us with your precious bundles for nine-plus hours a day, you make learning a priority in your household, and you share our goal of college graduation for your children.

To the staff at Success Academy in the network and back offices—you are the unsung heroes. You make this work possible through your focus on efficacy, efficiency, and innovation, and through your commitment to delivering services to children better today than you did yesterday.

We are deeply grateful to the educators in schools across the country who have so generously shared their wisdom with us, and to the reformers who have put fixing public education front and center in the American public debate.

Most important, Eva is grateful to her husband, Eric Grannis, and three kids, Culver, Dillon, and Hannah, who inspire her to run world-class schools, and Arin to her husband, Troy Lavinia, and son, James, who provide unflagging support.

ABOUT THE AUTHORS

Eva Moskowitz, a product of the New York City public school system and a public school parent herself, is founder and CEO of Success Academy Charter Schools, which will operate fourteen public charter schools in New York City as of August 2012. Her first school, Success Academy Harlem 1, founded in August 2006, quickly emerged as one of the top-performing schools in New York State, ranked by the *New York Times* as number one in math among 3,500 public schools. The former three-term New York City Council member visited hundreds of schools as chairperson of the council's Education Committee and earned a national reputation as a fighter for improving schools' rigor and investing heavily in the arts, sports, and science instruction. Eva earned a PhD in history at Johns Hopkins University and taught history at the University of Virginia, Vanderbilt University, and the City University of New York. She is the author of *In Therapy We Trust: America's Obsession with Self-Fulfillment* (Johns Hopkins University Press). She and her husband, Eric Grannis, are the parents of Culver, Dillon, and Hannah.

Arin Lavinia is a former staff developer at Columbia University's Teachers College Reading and Writing Project, literacy consultant, and New York City public school teacher. She has worked to improve the quality of literacy instruction and teacher training both in New York City and nationally. She joined Success Academy as the network's first director of literacy in 2009. With Success Academy CEO and founder Eva Moskowitz, Arin has designed and developed THINK Literacy, a commonsense approach to balanced literacy that puts critical thinking front and center, as well as Success Academy's methods of training principals and teachers. She and her husband, Troy, are the parents of James.

INDEX